God's Radical Plan for Wives

Companion Bible Study

By Jennifer Edwards

God's Radical Plan for Wives—Companion Bible Study

©2014 Jennifer Edwards
First Edition

Published by Principles to Live By, Roseville CA 95661
www.ptlb.com

Cover by John Chase
Copyedited by Jennifer Edwards, Sandy Johnson

All rights reserved. No part of this publication may be reproduced, stored in a retrieval system, or transmitted in any way by any means—electronic, mechanical, photocopy, recording, or otherwise—without the prior permission of the copyright holder, except as provided by USA copyright law.

All Scripture verses are from the New American Standard Bible unless otherwise indicated. New American Standard Bible: 1995 update. 1995 La Habra, CA: The Lockman Foundation.

Due to the sensitive subject matter, names and other identifying information have been altered to protect the privacy of those whose stories and quotes are included in the book.

ISBN 978-0-9838602-2-8
Christian Living /Marriage

Printed in the United States of America

To Mike

*You're the reason I try to be a godly wife.
You deserve the best from me and I love you.*

To Gil & Dana Stieglitz

*Thank you for encouraging me to go further
than I would have on my own.
God is amazing!*

Table of Contents

ABOUT THE AUTHORS 7

A NOTE FROM THE AUTHORS 9

ABOUT THIS STUDY 11

INTRODUCTION, CHAPTER 1, AND CHAPTER 2 15

CHAPTER 3—RESPECT 25

CHAPTER 4—ADAPT 51

CHAPTER 5—DOMESTIC LEADERSHIP 85

CHAPTER 6—INTIMACY 111

CHAPTER 7—COMPANIONSHIP 135

CHAPTER 8—ATTRACTIVE SOUL & BODY 163

CHAPTER 9—LISTENING 193

CONCLUSION 217

APPENDIX 225
- THE FIVE PROBLEMS OF MARRIAGE CHART 227
- THE FIVE PROBLEMS OF MARRIAGE 229
- THE GODLY WIFE 231
- THE GODLY HUSBAND 233

LEADER'S GUIDE 235

USEFUL RESOURCES FOR MARRIAGE 269

OTHER RESOURCES 270

About the Authors

Gil Stieglitz is an inspirational author, counselor, speaker, and President/Founder of Principles to Live By. He is the author of over twenty books, including *Becoming a Godly Husband* and *Marital Intelligence*. A pastor and teacher for over thirty years, Gil has spent thousands of hours counseling couples in their marriages and has witnessed dramatic results in cases where the principles he teaches are applied. He is currently the Executive Pastor of Adventure Christian Church, an adjunct professor at Western Seminary, and a church consultant for Thriving Churches International. He received his Master of Divinity and Doctorate of Ministry degrees from Talbot School of Theology.

Dana Stieglitz has been wife to Gil for twenty-five years and is the mother of three beautiful girls. She is a nurse practitioner with a Bachelor's and Master's degree in nursing and is finishing her Doctorate in Nursing in 2014. She is a certified Stott Pilates Instructor and works at Kaiser Hospital in Roseville and Sacramento. Dana co-authored *God's Radical Plan for Wives (formerly Becoming a Godly Wife)* with her husband, offering her wisdom and insight into the work.

Gil and Dana portray a biblical example of what it takes to be a godly married couple. Applying Scripture and real-life examples, *God's Radical Plan for Wives* draws upon their own marital experiences over the last twenty-five years. Their hope and prayer is that their book, along with *God's Radical Plan for Wives Bible Study,* will help wives bring about real, positive change in their marriages. The Stieglitz family resides in northern California.

Jennifer Edwards is an author and Bible teacher whose passion is to help women understand the truth of God's Word and how it applies to their lives in practical, realistic ways. She firmly believes there is both power and peace when a woman embraces God's prescribed role of wife in a marriage, which led to the writing of *God's Radical Plan for Wives Bible Study Workbook.* Jennifer is a graduate student at Western Seminary, where she is earning a Master's degree in Biblical Studies and Theology. With her no-nonsense and transparent approach, she is a popular speaker and teacher, encouraging women to adopt *God's Radical Plan for Wives* using the principles highlighted in this book. She is an established editor and freelance writer, serving Christian authors and publishers. Married to Mike Edwards for twenty-two years, she is also mother to a teenage son and daughter. The Edwards Family resides in Loomis, California. Learn more about Jennifer and book her for speaking at www.jenniferedwards.net; for editing and writing, www.jedwardsediting.net.

A Note from the Authors

*"She chose to fight for the future of her family and for her husband.
She is a godly wife."* ~ Gil Stieglitz

The idea of becoming a godly wife might strike an unpleasant cord with some women. For one thing, what does being "godly" mean anyway, and is it still relevant today? The very idea of being a *godly wife* might seem a bit old-fashioned or outdated, possibly even a little too conservative. Many women may already feel they are doing everything for their husbands—they are "good enough" wives (surely any marital issues are his fault, right?). Yet the godly wife goes beyond "good enough." She gives the marriage everything she's got for the sake of those in her life.

Knowing what makes a marriage thrive is important. Granted, it takes two people to make it work. By taking the principles taught in *God's Radical Plan for Wives* and adapting it into a comprehensive Bible study, we have developed an instrument designed to instruct and guide you to be part of the solution to problems and conflict in your marriage. In a sense, you could say we are empowering you to fulfill God's role for you as a wife to make the marriage the best it can be as it pertains to you.

In this study you will learn things that may seem contrary to what our culture says about what to do, how to think, and feel. But don't be alarmed! God calls us to be wives of excellence and to be in the world, not of the world; and it will not always be easy to hear some of the things that may seem archaic to today's modern women. But knowing that God's ways and truths are timeless, we can trust that He knows what is best to make our most important (human) relationship succeed. When we surrender to Him and begin to apply His teachings and examples to our own marriages and relationships, lives are changed for the better and joy, intimacy, and peace are restored.

Following *God's Radical Plan for Wives* will come easier for some women than others. The way marriage was modeled early on is an important indicator for many couples as to whether or not a marriage will succeed. If you were lucky, you grew up in a home where your mother modeled the *godly wife* well. Perhaps your father understood how to love his wife as Jesus loved the church; and you grew up as a witness to a marriage built on love, trust, and commitment. Hopefully you saw them spending time together, touching and laughing, talking about future plans, or working through issues in a respectful, thoughtful manner. The give and take, edification, and mutual respect they had for each other were signs of a strong, faithful, and godly marriage.

Unfortunately, many didn't grow up that way. Perhaps you came from a home with a broken marriage filled with pain—a place of fighting and stress, a lack of mutual respect for each other, and broken promises. Perhaps one partner in the marriage gave up and left, or if they stayed together, an uncomfortable tension resided in the home most of the time. The good news is that their experience does not have to define yours. You can choose a different path; you can choose to follow God's R.A.D.I.C.A.L. plan for wives.

If being a radical, godly wife is not second nature to you, what can you do? You've come to the right place. Soon you will have the tools, resources, practical exercises, and all kinds of information necessary to foster your own successful, joy-filled marriage. We pray that you will engage the materials wholeheartedly and with purpose. They have made a difference to many women before you; and if you work hard, we're confident they will make a difference in your life as well. It won't take long for you and your husband to notice positive differences in the relationship. Soon your godly marriage will light the way for your own children, their children, and the lives of your friends, relatives, co-workers, and neighbors. Our hope is that this study will allow you to experience many years of "happily ever after."

Gil & Dana Stieglitz
Jennifer Edwards

About This Study

God's Radical Plan for Wives is ideal for any woman interested in having a godly marriage—you could be engaged, a newlywed, currently married, remarried, or even divorced. We realize that every marriage is different, each with its own challenges. Some are more complicated than others or are considered "non-traditional." It doesn't matter if you are younger or older, married for one year or thirty, we are confident you'll experience positive changes in your marriage after you spend a little time and effort doing the work and applying what you learn. Like anything in life, when effort is put into something, there are big rewards. Fortunately, commitment to this study will pay off with a rich, rewarding marriage that benefits many.

We have seen many women make a positive difference in their marriages when they applied the principles from *God's Radical Plan for Wives*. Women at all stages of life and marriage have attended our workshops and classes. Some, whose marriages were struggling or even on the brink of divorce, have experienced healing as they applied what they learned. Women who experienced divorce have attended hoping to learn something different so they won't make the same mistakes the next time around. Even women married for thirty-plus years have gleaned new insights and were able to breathe life back into their marriages. Young women new to married life came away equipped and prepared to be the best wives to their husbands as well as women in their mid-life who were facing a new phase of marriage without the kids. The principles taught in *God's Radical Plan for Wives* really work; we've seen it with our own eyes.

Format and Materials

The study can be done either as a personal study, in a group, or with a mentor. A Leader's Guide is provided at the back of the book to assist group leaders. Each of the nine lessons provides biblical teaching about God's design for marriage, combined with marriage exercises designed to equip you to meet the fundamental needs of your husband. A typical week is made up of five days of homework that take on average 30-45 minutes to complete. Extra time should be allotted for the marriage exercises sprinkled throughout the chapter. Each lesson corresponds to the book, *God's Radical Plan for Wives*, by Gil & Dana Stieglitz, and is necessary to complete the homework. You will also need a Bible, preferably a New International Version (or another that is easy-to-understand), as well as a dictionary. On-line resources include www.Biblegateway.com and www.merriam-webster.com, among others. A separate notebook or journal would be helpful to write out thoughts, ideas, feelings, insights, and results you experience on this journey.

In addition, we recommend having husbands read *God's Radical Plan for Husbands*, written for men interested in learning how to love his wife in a way that meets her deepest needs. Also, *Marital Intelligence: A Foolproof Guide to Saving and Strengthening Marriage*. These resources are also available on audio book. Building a good marriage is a lifetime process, and these books can be used as resources that can be revisited from time to time. Visit www.ptlb.com for more information.

Note: Some of the exercises are more involved than others and may be more beneficial to do together with your husband. As a student you will gain more from this study if you attempt to complete all of them at some point in your marriage. Don't feel like you have to do them all at once or in sequence. The important thing is to focus on one area of need at a time and master it. Once one need is mastered, prayerfully consider the next need to master, and so on.

Lesson One

Introduction

Chapter 1: The Wife Role

Chapter 2: Affecting Change

Lesson 1

Introduction, Chapter 1, and Chapter 2

Lesson one is designed to prepare you for the weeks ahead by getting some foundational background reading out of the way. The Introduction provides the story about how *God's Radical Plan for Wives* came about and gives you an idea about the heart and intention behind the development of the materials. Chapter 1, *The Wife Role,* discusses the full extent of God's intention for wives and how that has played out historically. Chapter 2, *Affecting Change,* will help you understand how meeting your husband's needs motivates him to be the best husband, father, employee, community leader, and so on, with your help and guidance. It will explain how meeting his needs can in turn be applied to meet your needs.

Before you begin, pray that God would open your heart and give you new insight into His ultimate plan for wives.

Day 1—Introduction

1. Read the Introduction in *God's Radical Plan for Wives*. Make notes in the margins or underline anything you're unclear about that could be discussed with your class or mentor.

2. What is your impression of the authors' hearts from the reading?

Marriage Takes Work

3. According to the reading, what does it mean to love someone? What do you think the author means by this?

4. What can happen to a marriage when a wife begins to meet the deepest needs in her husband?

Pathways to Marital Bliss

5. What are the two pathways to marital bliss?

6. Which one do you plan to follow?

The Top Needs of a Wife

7. What are the top needs of a wife? Beside each letter, write down a brief summary.

    H

    U

    S

    B

    A

    N

    D

8. Which ones do you feel your husband does a good job of meeting? Which ones could he use guidance in improving?

The Top Needs of a Husband

9. What are the top needs of a husband? Beside each letter, write down a brief summary.

   R

   A

   D

   I

   C

   A

   L

10. Which ones do you feel you do a good job of meeting? Which ones could you use guidance in improving?

Daily Wrap-Up

In your own words, finish this sentence as it pertains to today's lesson: "If I am to follow *God's Radical Plan for Marriage,* I need to work on..."

Think About This!

"As you act differently toward him and meet his deepest relational needs, he will be drawn toward you."

"Realize that a marriage is a long-term relationship of meeting each other's needs, enjoying one another, and working through the issues of two separate people trying to become one."

Day 2—Chapter 1

1. Read Chapter 1 in *God's Radical Plan for Wives*. Make notes in the margins or underline anything you're unclear about that could be discussed with your class or mentor.

2. Write down all of the roles you play in your life.

3. Which ones do you feel most proud of? Why?

4. Which ones are difficult for you? Why?

5. In what ways can a wife influence the people in her life in positive or negative ways?

6. Historically, how have the people in your life influenced your view of the "Wife Role"? (Consider your mom, grandmothers, aunts, friends, and so on.)

7. How is your view different? Why? What is the role of wife to you?

Daily Wrap-Up

In your own words, finish this sentence as it pertains to today's lesson: "If I am to follow *God's Radical Plan for Marriage,* I need to work on..."

> **Think About This!**
>
> "As you act differently toward him and meet his deepest relational needs, he will be drawn toward you."
>
> "Realize that a marriage is a long-term relationship of meeting each other's needs, enjoying one another, and working through the issues of two separate people trying to become one."

Day 3—Chapter 2

1. Read Chapter 2 in *God's Radical Plan for Wives*. Make notes in the margins or underline anything you're unclear about that could be discussed with your class or mentor.

2. How important is meeting your husband's deepest relational needs to his overall development as a man?

3. What is a biblical definition of love according to the reading? Is love something that just happens? How do feelings come into play?

4. How do you think the experiment with the dolphin and dolphin trainer could relate to meeting your husband's needs and getting your needs met as well?

Learning a New Language

5. Do you feel like you and your husband speak a different language sometimes? In what ways?

6. What positive things can you do to remove the mystery for him of what you want and need from him?

What are His Fish?

7. What does the reading say a husband's "fish" are?

8. What happens when he is rewarded with these? What ultimately happens to your relationship when these needs are met?

A Role that Benefits Everyone

9. What attitude should a husband and wife have toward their marriage relationship? How does it relate to the way an organization runs successfully?

10. Like Dana, do you have examples of times when you appreciated things your husband did even if they didn't meet your standards? How could you do more of this?

Daily Wrap-Up

In your own words, finish this sentence as it pertains to today's lesson: "If I am to follow *God's Radical Plan for Marriage,* I need to work on..."

Think About This!

"It is not demeaning to learn the rules of being a "wife" and then use them to build a great marriage. If she does that, she will be successful, and her husband and family will be successful, all for God's glory."

Weekly Wrap-Up

In your own words, finish this sentence as it pertains to this week's lessons: "If I am to follow *God's Radical Plan for Wives,* I need to work on...."

Day 1

Day 2

Day 3

What is the **#1 take-a-way** you had from this week's lesson?

Lesson 2

Chapter 3: Respect

Lesson 2

Chapter 3—Respect

The Energy He Needs

Who knew that two little words like *respect* and *admire* could have such a huge impact on one's marriage? A man's need for a woman's respect and admiration drives him to attempt and achieve what he cannot (or will not) do on his own. Many books have been written on this topic. That's because experts know *respect* is one of the most powerful tools any wife can employ to strengthen her marriage. *Respecting and admiring* your husband every day energizes him to reach his full, God-given potential. Ultimately this unlocks his ability to understand how to best meet *your* needs, which in turn can lead to a marriage that works—one where both partners are fulfilled and full of joy.

This week's lesson teaches about the importance of showing respect and admiration to your husband. It provides opportunities for you to practice demonstrating them in new ways each day. You may not know it yet but showing respect and admiration for your husband is where the "power" lies in fostering a great marriage. It may seem unnatural or uncomfortable at first, but as you practice what you learn, you will begin to notice changes in him—small at first or maybe even significant. If you want to jump-start a recovery in your marriage or strengthen what you already have, then learning to *show* respect to the man you married in a way that he *feels* respected is critical. Time spent on the following lessons, along with some patience and a little practice, can strengthen your marriage in powerful ways.

My Prayer For Him...

Heavenly Father, thank you for my husband and for allowing me to walk through life with him. Lord, you command me to respect my husband for my own good. Teach me what godly respect is and how to live it out in my marriage. Give me wisdom and the ability to show him the respect he needs in a way he receives it. May I always appreciate him fully and respect who he truly is.
In Jesus' Name,
Amen

Day 1—Understanding Respect: Part I

Today we will get an in-depth understanding of *respect* and how it looks in godly marriage.

1. Read pages 27-32 in *God's Radical Plan for Wives.*

2. Looking at the story of "Beth," what were some of her characteristics and traits?

3. Because of her actions toward Dave, how did she make him feel about her? Why?

4. In your Bible, look up the following verses and record what it says about the <u>attitude</u> and <u>actions</u> of the wife:
   a. Ephesians 5:33

   Is "respect" a suggestion or a command?

   b. Proverbs 12:4

   How might a wife "disgrace" her husband?

   c. Proverbs 19:13

   What does "quarrelsome" mean and what affect does it have on the husband?

5. According to your reading, write out what *respect* means. When you show respect, what do you acknowledge?

   To demonstrate respect, you can focus on your husband's:

   ➢ _____

   ➢ _____

   ➢ _____

   ➢ _____

   ➢ _____

6. Based on the reading, answer the following statements True (T) or False (F):

   _____ Respect can only be earned.

   _____ A man's need for respect is so great, he will do almost anything to fulfill it.

   _____ Respect means to act, speak, and refer to the valuable things in a person's life instead of pointing out mistakes, problems, and weaknesses.

   _____ Respecting your husband is optional for a healthy marriage.

   _____ Criticism and disrespect destroys the husband's motivation to love his wife.

   _____ A wife's chiding and nagging stimulates the desired reaction from her husband.

7. Check the words or phrases that best describe *respect*.

admiration	_____	criticizing	_____
negativity	_____	complimenting	_____
gossiping	_____	encouraging	_____
appreciation	_____	chiding	_____
showing approval	_____	shaming	_____
pointing out mistakes	_____	expressing worth	_____
finding value	_____	demeaning talk	_____

8. Check all the actions below that would demonstrate respect to your husband?
"I show respect for my husband when I…"
   - ☐ Listen to him
   - ☐ Care for his needs
   - ☐ Lie to cover up my spending
   - ☐ Give my time to him
   - ☐ Bestow titles and positive nicknames
   - ☐ Talk in a negative tone of voice
   - ☐ Talk with kindness and affirmation
   - ☐ Give things up for him
   - ☐ Dress nicely, take care of myself
   - ☐ Have a positive attitude towards him
   - ☐ Am interested in HIS topics
   - ☐ Demean his ideas, thoughts, and actions privately or in front of others
   - ☐ Complain about my life, house, family, and so on
   - ☐ Spend money on him appropriately
   - ☐ Compliment him on the great job he's doing/how hard he's working
   - ☐ Look at him with admiration, smile at him
   - ☐ Have a bad attitude
   - ☐ Continue what I'm doing while he's talking
   - ☐ Show concern about problems he's having
   - ☐ Pray for him regularly

9. From the examples above, can you identify any areas in the way you relate to your husband? Consider and record some ways you could change disrespectful actions into ones that are more respectful.

Daily Wrap-Up
In your own words, finish this sentence as it pertains to today's lesson: "If I am to follow *God's Radical Plan for Marriage,* I need to work on..."

> **Think About This!**
>
> "Respect is the energy he needs to grow into all the man he can be."
>
> "You are on an assignment from God Himself to respect your husband."
>
> "A woman who criticizes and shows disrespect destroys her husband's motivation to love her."

Marriage Exercise #1

The Power of Paying a Compliment

Paying someone a compliment can give the verbal boost they need to get through a tough day. Spend time on today's exercise focusing on the strengths and successes of your husband. Below are three mini-assignments to complete throughout the week.

1. In a journal, notebook or the spaces provided, write down five things your husband does well. These would include his strengths, contributions, positions, accomplishments, and abilities.

    -
    -
    -
    -
    -

2. Commit to paying him a compliment about some of these strengths throughout the week. Say something like, "Honey, I've noticed you are really good at…" or "The way you do ____ really makes sense (or makes a difference by….)."

3. Select one of his special abilities and write him a postcard, note, or e-mail expressing your appreciation of that quality and how it positively impacts you and the family. It can be a quick gesture or perhaps a love note. Use your creativity.

Journal: What did you do? How did your husband respond? Were there any changes you noticed in his behavior toward you?

Day 2—Understanding Respect: Part II

A man has several sources in his life that provide the respect he desires. These include, but are not limited to, his family, work, hobbies, neighborhood, church, and so on. As his wife, he needs you to be the *steady* source of respect he can count on to remind him of his value. When you do this, it gives him the energy he needs to be able to tackle the challenges in his life. In other words, when you become the supplier of a steady diet of the very thing that sustains him (respect), you are invaluable to him. Let's discover how to do this well.

1. Read pages 32-39 in *God's Radical Plan for Wives.*

2. As it pertains to your husband's life, what are some of his sources of respect?

3. What are possible risks that come when respect is withheld?

4. To further define the meaning of the word *respect,* take a look at Ephesians 5:33 in the *Amplified Bible Translation* shown below. Use a dictionary to look up the definition for each of the underlined words. Make sure to observe the correct part of speech (verbs). Also, take notice of the synonyms associated with each word. Record what you find on the lines provided. This might seem like a lot of words to look up; but trust me, there is a point to it. (You might want to use an on-line dictionary to save time.)

   "... And let the wife see that she respects her husband—that she notices him, regards him, honors him, prefers him, venerates and esteems him, and that she defers to him, and praises him, and loves and admires him exceedingly."

   To show respect is to...

   Notice:

   Regard/Honor:

Prefer:

Esteem/Venerate:

Defer:

Praise:

Love:

Admire:

Exceedingly:

5. Using the definitions, write a personalized statement of what it would look like to show respect to your husband.

   This is how I can show respect to (husband's name):

6. Define the following terms in your own words. Is this something your husband could be suffering from? Explain your answer.

   "Father Wound"

"Mother Wound"

"Wife Wound"

Daily Wrap-Up
In your own words, finish this sentence as it pertains to today's lesson: "If I am to follow *God's Radical Plan for Wives,* I need to work on…."

Think About This!

"If key people in your life regularly let you know how valuable you are, it gives you energy to tackle the challenges in your life. So it is with your husband."

"Your respect is what gives him the energy and desire to please you."

"A man needs to hear '*You done good*' every day."

Marriage Exercise #2

Changes To Make

Hopefully, you are beginning to realize that respecting your husband is crucial to a great marriage. It's possible that changes may need to be made, which can begin by taking an honest assessment of yourself as it pertains to how well you show respect to your husband. This exercise can help you identify weak areas to strengthen and good areas you are already doing to celebrate. Answer the questions below to the best of your ability. Record what you learn on the spaces provided.

1. Is there something you should be doing (that you currently are not doing) <u>to demonstrate respect</u> for your husband?

2. Is there something you should stop doing (that you currently are doing) that demonstrates a <u>lack of respect</u> for your husband?

3. What things are you doing that show your husband respect?

4. On a scale of 1 to 10, rate yourself in terms of how well you respect your husband (1 = complete lack of respect for your husband; 10 = completely respect your husband). Try to be honest even though it may be difficult.

    1   2   3   4   5   6   7   8   9   10

5. If you put down a rating between 1-6, why do you think you feel that way? What factors may contribute to this? What can you change or do differently? Remember, you can't fix or control what anyone else does but you. Think about what you can control and fix.

Day 3—Learning to Respect Him

Many wives feel that they have a part in making their husband perfect. In other words, if they just helped him improve in a couple of areas where he is deficient, they would have a good husband. If this sounds familiar to you, keep in mind that your husband married you because he thought you accepted him and loved him just the way he was. It goes both ways, doesn't it? If you focus on changing his deficient areas rather than on what he does well, there can be resistance and conflict that may eventually lead to pain and resentment on both sides.

Begin looking for reasons to praise him, to really revel in his masculinity and manhood. This is the only way to give him the *ENERGY* he needs to even consider changing his weaker areas. If he believes in his heart that you respect him even with all his faults, he will listen to your thoughts about areas to work on in order to be even more successful in the world and even more wonderful in your eyes. Today we will look at six areas of focus that can help to deepen the level of respect you have for your husband.

1. Read pages 39-53 in the *God's Radical Plan for Wives* book.

#1 Focus on what he does well.

He has a certain number of abilities, talents, strengths, and gifts and a huge need to be complimented, valued, and compensated for them. If he is going to make the changes necessary to achieve his greatest potential, it will be because the people closest to him energize him through respect when they focus on what he does well.

2. What are five things your husband does really well?

#2 Seek out his strengths.

What are his obvious strengths? Be as specific as possible. Don't just write down that your husband is smart; rather, specify his intelligence: "He knows a lot about politics, he knows how to run a profitable business, or he knows a lot about _____." Stay away from any negatives, like the fact that he would look really good if he dropped 20 lbs. If something is a weakness, leave it off the list. Use these categories as a guide to spur your thinking. Complete the exercise below:

3. Physically: Looks, stamina, sleep, energy, strength, height, weight, health, and so on.

4. Emotionally: Justice, mercy, love, tenderness, joy, ability to overcome, kindness, steady, not over-reactionary, and so on.

5. Mentally: bright, memory, education, curious, wealth of knowledge, wisdom, creative, intuitive, and so on.

6. Spiritually: connected to God, awareness, moral, sensitive conscience, and so on.

7. Look at the relationships of his life. Which ones are blooming? In what areas is he strong? God/Spirituality, Personal Development, Marriage, Family, Work, Church/Community of Faith, Community, Money, Friends

#3 **Inventory his important accomplishments.**
8. Complete Marriage Exercise #3.

#4 **Figure out what he refrains from or avoids doing?**
Had you ever thought to praise your husband for things he *doesn't* do? Sometimes it is helpful to understand what he is refraining from – either at work or in the neighborhood. Women might take these things for granted as part of normal behavior. But to a man, *not* doing something they *could* be doing is something to be congratulated for!

9. Take a look at the examples below and check the ones your husband refrains from doing (that you know of). After you review your answers, spend some time in prayer thanking God for the good choices he has made in avoiding certain things. Then pray for strength in the areas where he may be weak.

35

"Thankfully, my husband avoids":

- ☐ Getting drunk/excessive use of alcohol
- ☐ Using drugs
- ☐ Viewing pornography
- ☐ Affairs with other women
- ☐ Yelling at the kids and me
- ☐ Frequenting strip clubs
- ☐ Swearing or cursing
- ☐ Overspending
- ☐ Bad behaviors at work/fired from his job
- ☐ Laziness or sloth
- ☐ Pride, large ego, or arrogance
- ☐ Expecting me to pick up after him
- ☐ Fighting
- ☐ Belligerent conduct
- ☐ Gambling, on-line or at a casino
- ☐ Unsafe driving
- ☐ Loud, unruly friends
- ☐ Activities or hobbies that exclude the family; like video games, technology, excessive involvement in outside activities, hobbies
- ☐ Lying
- ☐ Violence, rage, anger
- ☐ Watching too many sports shows

#5 Appreciate his spiritual gifts.

God bestows special abilities and areas of giftedness on people as they begin their relationship with Jesus Christ. The gifts are to be used by Christians to help others and the world in general to promote and serve the Kingdom of God. You can take an on-line spiritual gift assessment test to figure out where your gifts lie.

10. Looking over the list of Spiritual Gifts from the reading, list five gifts you think your husband might have or you may have observed in him. You may want to read 1 Corinthians 12-14 to get more information about each gift. Spend some time thanking God for giving your husband these gifts and that they would become a rich source of value in his life and the lives of others.

-
-
-
-
-

#6 Appreciate his personality traits & temperament.
11. Your husband's personality traits can be a wonderful source of praise. If you have extra time this week, pick up a temperament book at a local bookstore or find an on-line resource such as www.strengthsfinder.com to discover the strengths and weaknesses of your husband's temperament as well as your own. Of course, he has to be the one to fill out the answers. Opposite temperaments can attract each other, which can lead to tension in the relationship. Appreciate his strengths and see how they can stand out in his life. Celebrate the uniqueness each of you have and how your strengths and weaknesses complement each other.

Daily Wrap-Up

In your own words, finish this sentence as it pertains to today's lesson: "If I am to follow *God's Radical Plan for Wives,* I need to work on...."

Think About This!

"We gain strength to change when people accept us, respect what we do, and love us."

"A wise woman helps her husband celebrate his accomplishments, knowing that the celebration gives him energy to accomplish more."

"Many men are respectable for what they *don't* do."

Marriage Exercise #3
Accomplishments Inventory

Today ask your husband about his *top five accomplishments*. All men have accomplishments they are proud of that actually allow him to carry on in his life. Often men answer, "marrying you" as their greatest accomplishment. How sweet, right? It could also be having children, a trip he took the family on, or keeping a job for 5+ years. They could also be something that happened in elementary, middle, or high school. You may not realize it, but until he has more recent accomplishments, those from his past will not fade into the background. They are important to him!

Help him think of other things he accomplished either by himself, had help with, or was part of the process. Which is the one he is most sentimental about? Avoid comparing his accomplishments to those of others. The fact that he accomplished something is significant and you want to be careful not to cheapen it. The categories listed below will prompt you to think about areas that might not normally come to mind. Record what you learn in your journal or the spaces provided below. Reflect on what you learn about him.

- Projects (home, work, community, neighborhood, side jobs, repairs made)
- Paychecks (size, number, consistency, savings, growth)
- Workplace (positions, titles, promotions, skills developed or demonstrated)
- Vacations (trips, destinations, memories, expenses)
- Military (honors, service, life-changing experiences)
- Education (degrees earned, honors, schools attended, classes taken)
- Athletics (teams, triumphs, championships, achievements, awards, trophies)
- Writings (notes, letters, articles, books)
- Speaking engagements (speeches, presentations, lectures)
- Purchases (self, home, family)
- Community involvement (responsibilities, positions, accomplishments)
- Charity (help offered to others, comfort given in crisis)
- Impactful conversations (children, spouses, colleagues, friends, others)

Accomplishment #1

Accomplishment #2

Accomplishment #3

Accomplishment #4

Accomplishment #5

What am I most proud of my husband for?

Day 4—Get Real (Expectations)!

Expectations are funny things. An expectation is a belief that something should happen in a particular way, or that someone or something should have particular qualities or behaviors. As women, we generally have high expectations of ourselves to do things a certain way or achieve certain things in our lives. It is common to push some of these same high standards on the people in our family, even to the point that our own value (as wives, mothers, and women) depends on whether those standards are met or not. When we experience anger, frustration, depression, or conflict around the home (or anywhere really), it is a good idea to review our expectations. There might need to be some compromise or lowering of expectations, if even just temporarily.

While it is fair to have certain requirements for our husbands or kids to help out around the house, comply with certain rules, or adhere to given responsibilities, many times we expect more than what is even possible from them at their age, stage of life, or busyness level. For example, if your husband has a stressful job with long hours or a long commute, your expectation for him to get busy with tasks at home when he walks in the door is probably too high. If you expect your kids to do lists of chores around the house; but they are very involved with school, sports, and activities, then you may be expecting too much from them if you factor in homework, time to rest, and to just be kids.

It's tricky for husbands. They are sometimes met with our cold, icy glares or cutting, critical words and don't understand why. Chances are they didn't meet one of our expectations. Is it unrealistic to expect your husband to read your mind about the things you need him to do? Should he be able to anticipate what would make the date, vacation, or special occasion perfect according to our standards? Is he supposed to notice the dirty dishes piled in the sink, or that the garbage needs to be taken out without reminding him? Some husbands do these things naturally, and others…well, they don't. Thankfully, there are ways we can get them do the things we need them to do in a godly way, which is the goal of this book.

1. Read pages 53-61 in the *God's Radical Plan for Wives* book.

2. How important are the expectations that we put on other people. What positive things can they produce? What negative things can they produce? Are there unmet expectations in your marriage? What are they?

3. How do you know if your expectations are realistic or not?

4. Think about the expectations you have for your husband in the areas of home, marriage, family-time, church, community, work, social time/recreation, and special occasions. Record your *met or unmet expectations* in the chart below.

Expectations	Met	Unmet
Home		
Marriage		
Family Time		
Church		
Community		
Work		
Social/Recreation		
Special Occasions		

5. Evaluate the unmet expectations and consider if they are reasonable or too high. Which unmet needs are really important to you and which are those you can compromise?

6. Are you willing to accept him as he is and forgive him if he is just not able to meet your expectations? Why or why not? Spend some time in prayer about this and ask God to give you a new perspective and the ability to love him the way God does.

7. *True* or *False*.

   _____ The quicker you are able to adapt your expectations for what your husband is really capable of, the faster your respect for him will grow and the stronger his love for you will be.

   _____ Leadership is getting others to accomplish your externalized expectations.

   _____ Criticism usually always brings about the desired results to get people to change.

   _____ Change takes time. In order to get past negative behaviors, begin by describing the positive behavior clearly and concisely that is needed from your husband.

   _____ Lowering your expectations for his capabilities means admitting to having to do everything yourself in order to get things done around the house.

8. Using your dictionary, define the words below and jot down any synonyms you find for each. Write down how they might affect positive change.

   Critic/Criticism:

   Sarcasm:

9. Use what you've learned this week about using *praise*, *compliments*, and *respect* to move your husband toward your reasonable expectations. Beside each negative response, practice *direct*, *positive,* and *pointed* responses.

   a. "I'm sick and tired of you leaving your dirty dishes all over the house! I'm not your mother!"

b. "Whenever we go out, it would sure be nice if you could treat me like I deserve to be treated!"

c. "I hate it when you just sit in front of the T.V. all night, clicking through the stations! It's like I'm not even here!"

d. "Every time the kids need something, you look at me like I'm the only one who can do it. You're their parent too!"

e. "I hate those stupid video games. Stop playing them and help me."

Daily Wrap-Up

In your own words, finish this sentence as it pertains to today's lesson: "If I am to follow *God's Radical Plan for Wives*, I need to work on…."

Marriage Exercise #4

> **Think About This!**
>
> "The quicker you learn how to adapt your expectations to what he is really capable of, the faster your respect for him will grow, and the stronger his love for you will be."
>
> "It is best to be direct, positive, and pointed in requesting a change rather than indirect, negative, and general."
>
> "Criticism does not work; neither does demanding and ranting."

A Man Needs A Woman Who Says Things Like...

Think of three examples to share for each expression below. Plan to compliment your husband for some of these things and enjoy his reaction. Don't worry! The first one might take him by surprise, or maybe he won't react the way you hope. But keep trying and be ready to expand on what you mean if he asks.

- *"I was just thinking of all the things you could do, but don't do…Thanks!"*

- *"I was just thinking of all the things you've done in your life…Amazing!"*

- *"I was just thinking of all the things you've done for me…you're the best!"*

- *"I was just thinking of all the things you've done for the kids…you're a great father!"*

Other:

"I was just thinking of all the ways you've let God use you…Praise God!"

"I was just thinking of all ways you're wired so uniquely…you're amazing!"

"I was just thinking of all the skills/special abilities you have… you are wonderful!"

Day 5—Differences in Men and How They Receive Respect

All men are different, so it is safe to say that the way they receive respect varies, too. There are some men who will never be great conversationalists, and those who are incurable romantics. Some are intense in everything they do, while some are more relaxed and laid-back. You can help your husband develop his strengths by appreciating the positive areas of his life in the way he receives it best. Let's take a closer look at this.

1. Read pages 61-68 in the *God's Radical Plan for Wives* book.

2. From the reading, write a brief description for each personality type and what a man with this personality needs in order to feel respected:

   a. Strong, Dominant, Activist, Natural Leader:

   b. Life-of-the-Party Extrovert:

   c. Reserved and Pleasant:

   d. Highly Creative and Analytic:

3. Consider your husband. Which one best applies to him and why? (Could be a combination.)

4. Take a few minutes and write out how best you can show appreciation and love for your husband given his personality type. What do you do to show appreciation now? What can you begin to do? What do you need to change?

5. What can be the result in marriage when a woman allows herself to be disrespected or devalued? How important is it to establish and keep boundaries in a relationship?

Daily Wrap-Up
In your own words, finish this sentence as it pertains to today's lesson: "If I am to follow *God's Radical Plan for Wives,* I need to work on…."

Marriage Exercise #5
How Have His Experiences Shaped Him?

Use this exercise as a journaling exercise. You may want to go through it with your husband to get a better understanding about the important events in his life.

1. What happened to him from 0-5 years of age?

2. What happened to him from 5-10 years of age?
   - At home
   - In School

3. What happened to him from 10-15 years of age?
   - At home
   - In school
   - With friends

4. What happened to him from 15-20 years of age?
   - At home
   - In school
   - With friends
   - With the opposite sex
   - At church

5. What happened to him from 20-30 years of age?
   - At home
   - In school
   - With friends
   - With the opposite sex
   - At work
   - At church
   - Financially

6. What happened to him from 30-40 years of age?
   - At home
   - In school
   - With friends
   - With the opposite sex
   - At work
   - At church
   - Financially

7. What happened to him from 40-50 years of age?
   - At home
   - In school
   - With friends
   - With the opposite sex
   - At work
   - At church
   - Financially
   - Physically

8. What happened to him from 50-60 years of age?
   - At home
   - In school
   - With friends
   - With the opposite sex
   - At work
   - At church
   - Financially
   - Physically

9. What happened to him from 60-70 years of age?
   - At home
   - In school
   - With friends
   - With the opposite sex
   - At work
   - At church
   - Financially
   - Physically

Weekly Wrap-Up
In your own words, finish this sentence as it pertains to this week's lessons: "If I am to follow *God's Radical Plan for Wives,* I need to work on...."

Day 1

Day 2

Day 3

Day 4

Day 5

What is the **#1 take-a-way** you had from this week's lesson?

Lesson 3

Chapter 4: Adapt

Lesson 3

Chapter 4—Adapt
Creating Harmony

There are many truths about the man you married – not all of which you knew about when you agreed to marry him. Regardless of this, he is desperate for you to accept him just the way he is. He needs you to accept him as "your man" and embrace him completely—the good, the bad, and the ugly. After all, your husband is not perfect, but neither are you! He has flaws, defects, and weaknesses as well as wonderful strengths and potential. To be a truly great man, he needs you to adapt to the whole of who he is. As one friend pointed out to me, "Christ accepts us as imperfect, so why do we demand our husbands to be perfect?" That's a great question! When the "auto-adapting feature of dating" wears off, you have to determine what kind of marriage you want to have. Do you want a peaceful, harmonious marriage or one filled with competition and strife? It's a choice every wife has to make at some point in her marriage.

It's completely natural in marriage for a wife's acceptance and deference toward her husband to wane a little bit. If you have been married for a while, you may find that adapting to him takes a lot of work right now. You know his flaws and you continually find new things that bother you or are annoying. Maybe you notice his "lack of" in areas like social aptitude or helping around the house. All of that is normal. Adapting your life to fit his is not easy. In fact, it can be the hardest, most sacrificial work in marriage you will ever do.

This week's lessons are designed to give you a greater understanding of "the man" you married, including his weaknesses (which undoubtedly you are fully aware of already) along with his strengths. You will be asked to consider your own strengths and weaknesses, too, in order to determine areas that complement his. We will also cover the concept of *biblical submission*. I encourage you to go into this lesson with an open mind and heart, understanding that God is good and wants good things for us.

Proverbs 14:1 says, "The wise woman builds her house, but with her own hands the foolish one tears hers down." It is safe to say that a woman who refuses to adapt to her husband is capable of destroying her marriage all by herself. Let's look at adaptation in this week's lessons.

A Prayer For Him...

Heavenly Father, thank you for my husband and all of the ways you have blessed him. You've given him some amazing strengths that made him into the man he is. Please help me to see him as You see him and accept his weak areas. Give me wisdom to know how I need to adapt to him, and how I can come alongside him to help. In the areas that I am resentful or struggling to adapt, soften my heart so that I can be the wife you desire me to be.
In Jesus' Name,
Amen

Day 1—The Importance and Meaning of Adaptation

1. First, read pages 69-76 in *God's Radical Plan for Wives*.

2. Looking at the story of "Shelia," how do you relate to her situation? Are there ways you wish your husband was "more" or "less"?

3. Look up the following words to gain a deeper level of understanding of what "to adapt," means. Make sure to select the definition that best fits our subject matter—*adapting our behavior to fit the needs of our husbands*.
   To adapt:

   To complement:

   To accept:

Relational Peace & Harmony
Peace is not the absence of conflict. Like music, peace in a marriage occurs when two powerful and dynamic instruments play their notes in such a way that is harmonious and beautiful. The new melody (your marriage) is different and more creative than music played from either of the instruments individually (when you were single). The best marriages require the best qualities from both partners.

4. To more fully understand this idea, look up the following words.

   Peace:

   Dynamic:

   Harmony:

   Cacophony:

5. Visualize your household as a place of peace and harmony. Determine your part in making that happen. What would it take to live with your husband peacefully? What would life look like if the other person were declared the "winner" and conflict was put away?

   a. If you think of your marriage as music, describe what it would sound like? Is it harmonious or a cacophony?

   b. What do you want your marriage to be like? What is your goal?

6. From the reading, answer the following statements True (T) or False (F):

   _____ The goal of marriage is for each individual to outshine, out-do, or outperform the other in some or all ways.

   _____ Being a friend to your husband means bringing out his positive attributes and helping him hide or minimize his negatives.

   _____ The focus of marriage should be on personal happiness.

   _____ God commands wives to adapt to their husbands because it is one of his greatest relational needs. (*Ephesians 5:22*)

   _____ Marriage is like an orchestra. When one's notes don't blend with the other's notes, their symphony becomes a cacophony and is painful for all to hear.

Assessing Strengths and Weaknesses

A wise wife takes an honest look at herself and her husband and figures out where each of their strengths and weaknesses lie. Where he is lacking, she fills in those areas herself. Likewise, she guides him to fill in the areas where he is stronger and she is weaker.

7. List some of his strengths in **Column 1** and your weaknesses in **Column 2**.

Column 1 **His Strengths**	Column 2 **Your Weaknesses**

8. Now list <u>your</u> strengths in **Column 3** and <u>his</u> weaknesses in **Column 4**.

Column 3 **Your Strengths**	Column 4 **His Weaknesses**

9. Compare the columns. Are there areas where his strengths match your weaknesses, or his weaknesses match your strengths? Draw a line between those areas in Columns 1 and 2, then in Columns 3 and 4. Document those that complement each other below.

10. How can you apply your findings to your household? For example, let's say you are stronger socially and organizationally than he. You can see that your strengths would be useful in scheduling social times or outings. If this is the case, you might want to take ownership of scheduling social times as a couple.

11. How have you adapted to him in your marriage? How has he adapted to you?

12. Are there areas of friction that need to be smoothed out? Where should you adapt? What do you not like adapting to?

13. Ask yourself, "If I were to really adapt to him…if I were really going to make him successful…if I were really going to have a great marriage…what must I do?"

Daily Wrap-Up
In your own words, finish this sentence as it pertains to today's lesson: "If I am to follow *God's Radical Plan for Wives,* I need to work on…."

Day 2—You Were Designed to Complement Him (Part I)

In the beginning when two became one, an entirely new entity was formed. You, with your own set of unique gifts, talents, and skills, were put together with those of your husband to form a new life, a new team. As Christians, the mission of your team is to mature in Christ's likeness, righteousness, and holiness (Ephesians 4:24, 5:25-27). The trick is to figure out how to make this new team (marriage) work in the best way for everyone, so that it can be productive, healthy, and long-lasting. God fashioned men and women to be spiritual companions – two people who complement each other for good. With God, the three of you are a perfect, complete team.

This part of the lesson gets sticky for many of today's modern women. As daughters and granddaughters of brave women who grew up fighting for equality with men, we don't like or appreciate the idea of submitting to our husbands at all. Even the very word "submission" sends shivers down our spine. Our faces grimace with disdain and contempt. I believe we get anxious about the idea of submitting to our husbands for a few reasons: 1) we have seen how others pervert and misapply submission in harmful ways, 2) we are afraid to go backwards in history, 3) we only understand submission from the world's point of view, and 4) we don't truly understand the biblical reason for submission as it relates to God's design for marriage and how husbands and wives should relate.

Before we begin, try to set your preconceived ideas and thoughts about the *culture's definition* of submission aside for a little while as you attempt to understand biblical submission. My hope is that God will bring you to a place where you see His purpose in it and decide it's not so bad after all. Perhaps, it is actually good for us!

Though submission can be hard, it is necessary. God usually commands us to do what we don't naturally already do. He teaches us those things that are needed, beneficial, and good for us. When God designed the union of the man and wife, He created the man to lead his family; it's hardwired into his very being. As the leader, husbands have a huge need for their wives and family to adapt (submit) to him so they can lead effectively. Wives were asked by God to follow and are thus designed to complement and come alongside in this effort called marriage and family. Together, both of you can accomplish God's purpose and plan for your family.

My Prayer for You...

Dear Lord, this is a difficult topic for us wives. Work in our hearts and minds to help us understand your idea of biblical submission. Break down cultural and generational barriers or mind-sets that we have been taught in the past. Help us to see a different way — your way—that leads to a healthy marriage relationship. Please bless our efforts as we go through this lesson.
In Jesus' Name,
Amen

1. Read pages 76-78 in *God's Radical Plan for Wives*.

Biblical Submission

2. In your Bible, read Ephesians 5:22-6:9. Answer the following questions:

Wives are to:

    How?

    Why?

Husbands are to:

    How?

    Why?

Reading all of the passage, does God call for only wives to be submissive?

Who else is to be submissive? How?

How does God demonstrate submission? (*See also Philippians 2:1-11*).

3. Look up Colossians 3:18-19
   Wives are to:

   Husbands are to:

4. Look up 1 Peter 3:1-7. *Note: This speaks of submission in terms of roles or functions necessary for the orderly operation of society and the home.*
   Wives are to:

Husbands are to:

5. Titus 2:5
   Wives are to:

6. Look up the following words in your dictionary and write down the meanings, along with synonyms.
   Submit

   Defer

   Yield

   Voluntarily

7. The Greek word for "submission" is the word "*hupotasso.*" This word means a *voluntary submission*, a *yielding of one's self voluntarily*. It also means "to line up" or "to put in order under." This makes sense if we understand the order of authority in God's design for marriage. It looks like this: (see 1 Corinthians 11:3)

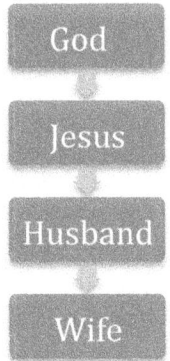

8. In God's created order, what is it that God commands wives to do?

58

9. How might voluntary submission to your husband's leadership be related to respect?

10. What might be some advantages to deferring or submitting to your husband?

11. What are some of your fears or reservations about submitting to your husband?

EXTRA: Your husband is commanded to love you as Christ loves the church. According to Philippians 2:1-15 and 1 Corinthians 13, describe in your own words what that means.

Daily Wrap-Up

In your own words, finish this sentence as it pertains to today's lesson: "If I am to follow *God's Radical Plan for Wives*, I need to work on…."

Think About This!

God's design for marriage can be summed up as: "Wifely submission balanced with loving, sacrificial headship from the husband."

"The key to helping your husband become all God created him to be requires your voluntary submission to his leadership. It is a major aspect of respect."

Day 3—You Were Designed to Complement Him (Part II)

1. From the standpoint of adapting and complementing one another, let's dig further to understand God's plan for marriage *before* the introduction of sin in the world. In your Bible, **read Genesis 2:4-25** and the account of the God-blessed union of Adam and Eve. Fill in the blanks below:
   a. What does Genesis 2:18 say?

   From this passage, what specific kind of helper did he provide to Adam? Why did God think he needed one?

   b. What does Genesis 2:22-25 say?

2. Just like Adam, God wants you to be a suitable helper to your husband! But what does being a "suitable helper" mean? In your dictionary, look up:
   Helper: *(Note: In Hebrew, the word "helper" is ezer meaning, "aid.")*

   Suitable: *(Note: The word "suitable" in Hebrew is "kenegdo," meaning, "corresponding to him" or "complementing him.")*

   The expression "*ezer kenegdo*" or "help-mate" means, "One who is the same as the other and who surrounds, protects, aids, helps, supports; a fitting helper for him." In other words, as his wife, we were chosen by God as his equal to come alongside him—to aid, help, and support him, so that he can achieve the full potential God has for his life, as well as your own life, through marriage.

3. Why is this so hard for us? Understand that it wasn't always that way. Let's take a look at the effect of sin on what was once a perfect marriage relationship.

   Read Genesis 3:1-16. This is the account of God's judgment on the serpent, the woman, and the man following Adam and Eve's sin in the Garden of Eden. Notice particularly verse 16. Write down the two curses that God gave the woman for her part in the sin.

   Consequence #1:

   Consequence #2:

   You see, God intended for Adam and Eve to enjoy the blessings of childbearing (Genesis 1:28) and a harmonious partnership in marriage (Genesis 2:18, 21-25). But because of sin, the consequences were great and far-reaching. Childbirth would still come but now with great pain. The harmony of the marriage relationship would now be challenged by the *woman's desire** to usurp the authority of her husband. It is her natural state. Knowing that at some point her desire to rule would clash with God's design for male leadership in marriage, God had to tell us the hard truth. The key to a great marriage is exercising voluntary submission. Otherwise, as women in our natural state, our selfishness and strong will can cause destruction in the marriage relationship.

   * In Genesis 3:16, the word "desire" in Hebrew texts is the same word used in Genesis 4:7 when it describes the desire sin had for Cain. It sought to enslave, possess, or control him. God commanded Cain to overpower sin and master it, implying there was an active struggle between sin's desire and Cain's will. This same word "desire" describes a wife's desire to possess or control her husband. Attempts to realign the order God created for marriage often causes conflict and pain because it is contrary to God's design for relating in a marriage. God designed men to be the head of their households; but because of sin, a husband's rule is challenged by a wife's natural tendency to have control.

4. Instead of relying on our own reasoning about God's call for our voluntary submission in marriage *(hupotasso)*, look again at what the Word of God says. **Using the verses you looked up in Day 2, answer the following questions.**

   The 5 "W's" and an "H" of Submission:

   What are we as wives to do?

   Who is to submit and to **Whom**?

When are we to submit?

Where are we to do this?

Why are we to submit?

How are we to submit?

How might this look in your own marriage?
No one said submission would be easy. In fact, it is because it is so difficult that God gave us this command! He only commands us to do those things that are needed, beneficial, and are not necessarily intuitive to our nature. He knows submitting isn't natural to our post-fall humanity as women; but He also knows with the power of Christ, it is possible (Mark 10:27).

5. Write how you can start exercising *hupotasso* in your marriage. Ask God to help you identify areas you can work on.

A Picture of Biblical Submission...

A healthy Christian marriage will exercise mutual consultation and the sharing of wisdom between husband and wife. For a wife to be submissive, it doesn't necessarily involve the obeying of actual commands or directives (unless they are vitally important for the health and safety of the family.) A husband will likely give requests, seek advice, and discuss the issue together with his wife to determine a course of action. A wife's attitude of submission to her husband's authority will be reflected in the words and actions each day that reflect a deference to his leadership and her support of his final responsibility for the family.

[1] Grudem, Wayne, and Piper, John, *Recovering Biblical Manhood and Womanhood.* Crossway: Wheaton, IL, 2006. Pg. *200.*

Daily Wrap-Up

In your own words, finish this sentence as it pertains to today's lesson: "If I am to follow *God's Radical Plan for Wives,* I need to work on…."

Think About This!

"Wives were chosen by God as his equal to come alongside him, to aid, help, and support him so that he can achieve the full potential God has for his life, as well as your own life through marriage."

"When you accept authority of your husband and decide to meet his deepest needs, you can change him into a caring, intimate person without talking about anything he's doing wrong."

Day 4—Adapting to Your Husband

Today's reading delves into the "How-Tos" of adapting to your husband. There are several areas where a wife can adapt—her expectations, his ideas, and his work, among others.

1. Read pages in 78-91 *God's Radical Plan for Wives*.

Dealing with Expectations
"Many wives must take a look at their expectations and adapt them to the truth of the person they really married."

2. Have you had any issues adapting your expectations to the truth of the man you married? If so, how?

Avoid Comparison

3. Has there ever been a time in your marriage when you compared your husband's abilities, talents, or skills to another person? How did that impact the way you viewed him?

How can you adapt to your husband?

4. Does adapting have anything to do with being the leader? Why or why not?

5. What is needed to make a marriage work?

6. What does it mean to "biblically adapt"?

Adapting to His Ideas

7. How important is it to incorporate your husband's ideas into the household?

8. List several ways you can adapt to your husband's ideas.

Adapting to His Work

It's no surprise that a man's work is a large part of who he is. In fact, he likely invests between eight to fifteen hours a day, five to seven days a week in it! Consequently, he also invests a considerable amount of time, energy, resources, and ego and self-worth to his work. God created man to enjoy work and often uses it as a way to find purpose and meaning in the world (Genesis 2:15). Hopefully your husband is thriving in his work and feels fulfilled in the work he contributes.

In order to have a successful marriage, it is imperative for a wife to understand the importance of work to her husband and also that she understands the particulars of his job and the complexities involved. You need to be willing to engage him about his work daily in order to touch the heart of your man. Your interest in the things that are most important to him will willingly keep him coming home to you.

9. How important is "work" to your husband?

10. How do you support your husband's job or handle work-related issues?

11. What things can you start doing to adapt more to his work?

Work is also very important to God. Let's look at the following verses in your Bible to glean an understanding of why work is so important to men and why your husband's work matters to God. Write down what you observe.

12. In the beginning, God gave work to man as a blessing, not a curse. Some think work is actually a form of punishment, but it isn't! God Himself is a worker as we can see in Genesis when He created the entire universe. In fact, John 5:17 tells us that God continues to be a worker. God's plan all along was to make work part of mankind's perfect existence. Look up the verses and record what they say.

Genesis 2:15

Genesis 3:17-19

How did work change after Adam and Eve disobeyed God?

13. Work is essential to a man's well-being. God created man with an emotional need that can only be met with an honest day's work. He longs to accomplish something and do valuable work. When he completes a difficult task, he feels satisfaction and a greater self-respect. (That's why it's so difficult for men when they lose their jobs or don't have one, or for recently retired men who have to find new things to do to make him feel valuable.)

Ecclesiastes 3:12-13

In what ways can work be a blessing (apart from financial gain)?

14. His job is a partnership with God. When he works, he is like a business partner with God in meeting the needs of his family and maybe even the world around him through generous giving. Needs to be met include food, clothing, shelter, protection, education, love, encouragement, and the furtherance of the saving knowledge of Jesus Christ. God uses people to fulfill those needs through work.

Exodus 35:30-36:1 – Note the different types of work commissioned:

15. God will judge your husband's work, as well as his motives, effort, integrity, and usefulness. All of it will be taken into account.

Ephesians 4:28

Colossians 3:23-24

2 Thessalonians 3:6-13 (Note: What does this verse also say about our job as wives?)

16. Given what you learned about God's design for work, reply to the following statements. Circle your answer.

    a. My husband is a hard worker.

    Most of the time   Some of the time   None of the time

    b. My husband works hard when he does something he enjoys.

    Most of the time   Some of the time   None of the time

    c. My husband finds fulfillment in his work.

    Most of the time   Some of the time   None of the time

    d. When he comes home from work he is excited to talk about the day's events.

    Most of the time   Some of the time   None of the time

    e. He considers work a blessing and a commission from God, rather than a necessary evil.

    Most of the time   Some of the time   None of the time

17. If you circled "none of the time" for any of the above statements, consider what things you could do to help your husband change his perspective or motivation.

Daily Wrap-Up
In your own words, finish this sentence as it pertains to today's lesson: "If I am to follow *God's Radical Plan for Wives,* I need to work on…."

Think About This!

"To biblically adapt means to figure out how to make the other person successful and what your part in the process entails."

"If a wife is going to build a great marriage, she must understand his work in all its complexities."

"His career is a huge part of who he is and what he is all about."

Marriage Exercise #3

Adapting To His Work

If your husband has a desire to do better at his job, get a promotion, or earn a certain amount of money, what would it take? First, take a look at what your husband currently spends his time doing. Fill out the weekly time schedule or ask him to fill it out with you. Make sure to incorporate time for family, exercising, worshipping God, recreation, drive time, resting, socializing, his marriage, and so on.

	6:00 a.m.	12:00 p.m.	6:00 p.m.	12:00 a.m.
Monday				
Tuesday				
Wednesday				
Thursday				
Friday				
Saturday				
Sunday				

Take a look at any areas that you could make easier for him in order to accomplish that level of involvement. What would need to change in his work schedule and private life?

	6:00 a.m.	12:00 p.m.	6:00 p.m.	12:00 a.m.
Monday				
Tuesday				
Wednesday				
Thursday				
Friday				
Saturday				
Sunday				

Note: As a couple, you need to take an honest assessment of the new schedule to see if it is realistic and something you both agree to. If the new schedule takes too much time away from the kids and home, you may want to re-evaluate. However, you may determine such a schedule is necessary short term to achieve certain goals.

Day 5—Adapting to His Leadership and More...

Good leadership is essential at every level of a successful organization. It is true that not everyone can be the leader, but did you know that God has gifted you as a wife to use your leadership abilities to accomplish the family's goals? As wives we are equipped with certain leadership skills, and we are required to use them especially in the areas where our husbands are weaker. When we do that, we get an opportunity to exercise our full leadership potential for the good of our marriage.

It might help to think of the household as a company. Your husband would be the CEO, while you would take on the role of manager. Both are responsible for the household; but the CEO's role provides direction, goals, and holds the ultimate authority for decisions made, while the manager is the one who generally makes things happen (whether by delegating, resourcing out, or doing it themselves). Both are leaders utilizing their skills and gifts.

1. Read pages 91-101 in *God's Radical Plan for Wives*.

Adapting to His Leadership

2. There are two myths in regard to leadership in marriage. What are they?

   -

   -

3. Answer "True" or "False" to the following statements about leadership:

   _____ "Leadership" is defined as others accomplishing your externalized expectations.

   _____ God doesn't believe women should be leaders. (In case you are unsure of your answer, read Judges 4 as it pertains to Deborah's role.)

   _____ The man's leadership at home is to be the hands-on director of all the activities of the home life.

   _____ The key to a great marriage is to realize that leadership in marriage is not the same as business, where ability displaces some and promotes others.

   _____ Both a husband and wife's leadership abilities must be combined to make sure both relationship and accomplishments are achieved.

   _____ Biblical submission means you take only a follower role, never exercising any leadership gifts or abilities.

   _____ Godly leadership does not demand power, attention, or position to exercise its energy. Rather it is humble, servant-oriented, and selfless.

4. In your home, each of you exercises leadership in certain areas. For example, one of you manages the finances, purchases the household good (groceries, supplies), negotiates with contractors or repairmen, takes out the garbage, or cleans the house/garage. Using these examples and other responsibilities within your own household, list who is the lead over the various areas in your home:

His	**Hers**

5. Are you content with the areas you each have leadership over? In other words, are you both leading in the areas that utilize your best abilities and uniqueness? What are some changes you could make so that the household could run more smoothly? Are there things you could take over from your husband to give him more time to do other things, such as spend time with the kids? What about him for you?

6. As women in today's post-modern culture, it is fairly common to resist her husband's leadership in the home. How about you? Do you resist your husband's leadership? If you think you may be guilty of any of these subtle forms of rejecting his leadership, make a check in the box next to it.

Do you:
- ☐ Take his discussions too personally
- ☐ Jump to conclusions about what he means or what it could mean to you
- ☐ Shut down his ideas too quickly
- ☐ Fail to look for the root intention
- ☐ Discount and ignore his ideas regularly
- ☐ Reject his ideas completely
- ☐ Make changes to his ideas too quickly
- ☐ Are only interested in discussing your ideas
- ☐ Only want to implement your ideas
- ☐ Believe that your vision for the family is the best one to be implemented

7. Consider any boxes you checked. In what ways can you draw him out and become more of a teammate with him? Record your answers in your journal or the lines below.

Adapting to His Personality

8. What are the strengths of his personality?

9. What are the weaknesses of his personality?

10. Think how you may need to adapt to his personality:

Adapting to His Phobias

11. In Gary Smalley's book *The DNA of Relationships*, he listed 25 fears that destroy marriages.[1] Look at the list and check which ones seem to animate him the most. If your marriage is at a place where you can discuss this list with him, ask him to suggest the ones that he considers to be his most dominant fears.

---

25 Fears That Destroys Marriage

- ☐ Rejection
- ☐ Judgment
- ☐ Disconnection
- ☐ Loneliness
- ☐ Failure
- ☐ Powerlessness
- ☐ Condemnation
- ☐ Feeling Unwanted
- ☐ Danger
- ☐ Being Misunderstood
- ☐ Being Scorned
- ☐ Being Invalidated
- ☐ Feeling Defective

- ☐ Inferiority
- ☐ Worthlessness
- ☐ Feeling Disliked
- ☐ Mistrust
- ☐ Despair
- ☐ Feeling Devalued
- ☐ Humiliation
- ☐ Abandonment
- ☐ Feeling Unimportant
- ☐ Feeling Ignored
- ☐ Neglect
- ☐ Unhappiness

---

12. How can you help allay these fears? What can you do to adapt to them? In other words, if you discover your husband is fearful of abandonment, what can you do to reassure him that you will not abandon him?

Adapting to His Background and Experiences

Every man had a series of good and bad experiences that have in some way shaped him into the man he is today. They can even be the reasons why he acts in certain ways. Write out any major positive or traumatic events in each period of his life that you are aware of. Go back and look at

---

[1] Smalley, Gary, *The DNA of Relationships*. Carol Stream, IL: Tyndale, 2004. Page 49.

the impact and power those events have had in his life. This is a good exercise for you to do for yourself as well.

Age Groups	**Major Positive or Traumatic Events**
0 - 10	
11 - 20	
21 – 30	
31 – 40	
41 – 50	
51 – 60	
61 – 70	
71 – 80	
81 - 90	

13. In what ways can you adapt to those events in his life? Determine if the power from those events still impact him today.

Adapting to His Culture or Heritage

When you married your husband, did you think about what culture or heritage background he had and all that comes with it? This could be his ethnic heritage, family heritage, and the surroundings or customs he grew up with.

14. Take a look at the list of areas in your family and write down things that seem right to him but maybe don't seem right to you. For example, dinner has to be at 5:00 p.m. Or, the woman is in charge of all the housework.

- Home

- Finances

- Children

- Friends

- Recreation

- Church

- Community Involvement

- Marriage

- Work

- Men's Roles

- Women's Roles

Over-adapting
15. What does it mean to over-adapt in marriage?

16. What are some examples of ways a wife can over-adapt to her husband?

17. Do you feel you are over-adapting in any way?

Note: If after reviewing this, you feel you may over-adapt in an unhealthy way, we recommend that you seek the advice of a pastor or godly counselor right away. This could include such actions as compromising your values or morals, allowing yourself to be denigrated or abused, or becoming involved in something illegal or perverted in order to keep the peace or avoid conflict. I would also recommend you become familiar with the terms "enabling" and "co-dependency" for your own knowledge. In the Bible, Acts 5:29 points to the limitations of adapting and submitting when it says, "We must obey God rather than men."

Daily Wrap-Up

In your own words, finish this sentence as it pertains to today's lesson: "If I am to follow *God's Radical Plan for Wives,* I need to work on…."

Think About This!

"After the wedding, you must adapt to a different set of values, ideas, standards and actions."

"The goal of marriage is to become a team that accomplishes good things for God, for the two of you, for the children and society."

"His lack of day-to-day management and detailed leadership does not mean he is not the leader."

Marriage Exercise #4

Adapting To His Leadership

Some men are maintainers, some initiators, while some are good at implementing the ideas of others. Some are good at managing, while others are good at refining an existing process. A man brings all he has into his marriage.

Unfortunately, some women may expect or want their husbands to be the exact kind of leader that they are, only better. While this isn't usually possible, it is wonderful to know that often God puts people together with strengths and weaknesses that complement each other. Let's take some time to figure out what kind of leader your husband is. What does he naturally express? Think about these questions and record your answers on the lines below.

1. If your husband were to be the leader of the following areas, what would it look like?
   - Home
   - Finances
   - Children
   - Friends
   - Recreation
   - Church
   - Community Involvement

2. What settings have you seen him take the lead?

3. How does he usually prefer to express his leadership? Directly (does things himself) or indirectly (through you and others)?

4. What kind of leader is your husband? Circle the one that best describes him. You may circle more than one. Refer back to the book for examples.

Initiator	vs.	Controller
Aggressive	vs.	Cautious
Personal (hands-on)	vs.	Delegating to others
Dominant	vs.	Laissez-faire
Upfront	vs.	Behind-the-Scenes

Marriage Exercise #5

Goal Setting

Goal Setting: This exercise has been very useful and beneficial in my marriage over the years. It helps us keep up with the goals we have for our family.

Like a successful company, you can have a household strategy meeting at the beginning of every year making goals and coming up with strategies for how to meet those goals. You can choose to meet annually (or even quarterly) to see how things are going. *Plan to set aside 2-3 hours – preferably without children – to brainstorm things pertaining to the success of your household.*

Categories might include:

- Home Improvements (inside and out)
- Children (#1, #2, #3, etc.)
- Marriage (How to keep it strong?)
- Finances (How are things going?)
- Vacations/Recreation Planning
- Friendships (Good, Bad, New, Old)
- Church (Attendance, Service, Tithing, Giving, Learning)
- Household Needs (Clothing, Furniture, Outdoors)
- Personal Wellness (Food, Fitness, Medical)

Weekly Wrap Up
In your own words, finish this sentence as it pertains to this week's lessons: "If I am to follow *God's Radical Plan for Wives,* I need to work on...."

Day 1:

Day 2:

Day 3:

Day 4:

Day 5:

What is the **#1 take-a-way** you had from this week's lesson?

Lesson 4

Chapter 5: Domestic Leadership

Lesson 4

Chapter 5—Domestic Leadership

The Heart of the Home

Before we delve into this important topic of domestic leadership, it's important to recognize that all women are different. We all have different ambitions, goals, skills, life situations, and ideas of what we want our lives to be like. With that in mind, our goal is to point you to what God says about the home and our role in it as wives. I trust that if you are reading this book, you are a wife who is seeking to understand a "godly" way of living as a wife. You are a woman who loves your husband and family enough to do the hard work in this workbook.

Women who take full-time care of the household have accepted this responsibility for one reason or another. The decision to focus on home may have been a set expectation from the beginning of the marriage, or the decision was made in order to maintain balance in the home. Though it can (and typically does) take an adjustment period to feel totally comfortable with this role of "stay-at-home mom," or "housewife," once you are in sync with the rhythms and flow of the home, it can be very fulfilling—a source of great joy, purpose, and meaning. Granted this may be only for a season of life or two, but the opportunity to focus on home is worthwhile.

While some women can choose to either quit their careers to stay home while the kids are young, other women either do not have that option due to financial reasons or they have strong career ambitions. Perhaps it's just what she knows or expects out of life. Working outside of the home may be very stimulating and rewarding while she does a job she loves. Not only that, she also makes a contribution to society and to her family by bringing home extra income. These women have the double role of managing their job and maintaining the household. It's not an easy way of life by any means.

In God's eyes, all women are valuable to Him for His purposes. Whatever your working situation, God designed the husband as the family leader but expects the wife to make her contribution in running the home and maintaining the peace. This chapter will give you godly insight into managing a home as it meets this important need in husbands.

My Prayer for You...

Dear Lord, Proverbs 16:3 says that when we commit our plans to you, they will succeed. We claim this verse today and ask for help by motivating us to take action for peace in our homes. Peace comes from you, Lord, and we want our homes to be filled with your peace, not confusion, noise, distraction, and strife of the outside world. Inspire us and give us courage to make hard choices if necessary. Amen

Day 1—The Need for Peace

Everyone experiences the pressure and strain from being out and about in the world on a daily basis. Demands, hassles, strife, traffic, personality conflicts, and deadlines can be exhausting, stirring a need for peace within each of us. The quote below summates this idea beautifully:

"When the pressures of the world intrude, there is no shelter like a peaceful home." ~ Author Unknown

In his crazy world, your husband is anxious to get home after a long day of work and the evening commute. With the increasing pressures of school activities and friendships, even children count on "home" to be the place of refuge and safety. Wives are also striving to meet the high expectations and demands of being a woman in today's culture and certainly desire a place of solitude and rest. What makes "home" so appealing? The goal is to make your home a place where your family, especially your husband, longs to be.

We're all familiar with quotes like, "Home is where the heart is," by Pliny the Elder and "There's no place like home," by Dorothy in *The Wizard of Oz*. They couldn't say it any better! If you really think about it, not all homes are appealing. Someone has to work very hard to make home a wonderful place. Truthfully and biblically, God has given wives this critical assignment to establish the *"heart"* of the home. When we create a place that promotes peace and refuge within its walls, our men come back to us at the end of every day and our children are content.

Men need to know with certainty that the "home front" is cared for. This is another deep-seated need of men and is met when his wife takes on the affairs of the home as the *domestic leader*. A man's longing to come home to a place that is well maintained and where the children are respectful and calm may seem very old-fashioned and outdated by today's standards. But old-fashioned or not, the need in men is still there. Men count on their wives to lead and manage domestic matters at home. Let's dig into this week's study to explore this idea further.

1. First, read pages 101-105 in *God's Radical Plan for Wives* book.

2. Looking at the story of "Bill and Sally," answer the following questions:

    a. What does Bill need in the home?

    b. What did Bill need Sally to do?

c. Describe how Sally spent her time. Why didn't she have enough time to meet the needs in the house? What did she discover to be true about the use of her time and her attitude regarding matters of the home? Can you relate to her in any way?

d. Was Bill's need unreasonable? Why or why not?

3. Look up the definition of the word *peace*. Record the meaning that best applies to *relationships* and *surroundings*.

4. Check the boxes that best describe the atmosphere in your home currently.

☐ Working together	☐ Laziness	☐ Busy
☐ Peace	☐ Helpful attitudes	☐ Active
☐ Yelling	☐ Organized	☐ Fast paced
☐ Disagreements	☐ Crazy	☐ Relaxed
☐ Clean	☐ Dirty	☐ Cooperation
☐ Noisy	☐ Disorganized/Cluttered	☐ Intentional
☐ Calm	☐ Pleasant	☐ Friendly
☐ Media noise	☐ Strife	☐ Warm
☐ Talking and relating	☐ Rigid	☐ Cold
☐ Laughter	☐ Well stocked/ abundance	☐ Flexible

5. Peace busters are things that take away peace in a surrounding. Write down any peace busters currently present in your home. Examples could be sarcasm or unkind words, too much activity, too busy, and so on.

6. Write down ten things you would like to change to promote peace in your home. Be mindful of the reality of your circumstances, such as the ages of your children, work schedules, personalities, and seasons of life. After that, brainstorm each point and think about how you can bring about the change you desire. Write down 1-2 tangible actions.

10 Desires for your Home	Action Steps to Get There
1.	
2.	
3.	
4.	
5.	
6.	
7.	
8.	
9.	
10.	

Daily Wrap-Up

In your own words, finish this sentence as it pertains to today's lesson: "If I am to follow *God's Radical Plan for Wives,* I need to work on...."

Think About This!

Always remember that God is a God of peace and desires the same for us in our lives. Pray over the vision you have for your household and ask for Him to help you make it a reality in your home. (Proverbs 16:3)

"When the children are under control and the house is inviting, he feels valued. Your husband is drawn to his home, his wife, and his children when there is relational peace."

"Your role as a godly wife in the home is vital to the enjoyment and long-term success of your marriage and family."

Marriage Exercise #1

Creating A Vision For Your Home

"Run a home like you would a small business and treat it with the same seriousness."
~ Anthea Turner

One of wisest, most valuable things a home leader does to keep the household running smoothly is to create a vision for the home, as well as for each member of the family. Deciding on a direction, setting goals, and establishing plans to get there are all pieces of the vision. Consider these questions and answer them to the best of your ability. You may need more time than you have today but don't give up! Revisit this page or create your own format on your computer. Complete all the questions if you can.

1. What changes can you make in yourself to attain to a higher level of domestic leadership? This can include changes in attitude, physical health, getting educated in an area where you are not as knowledgeable, trying something new, cutting your hours at work, and so on.

2. What does a successful home and family look like to you? How is the current situation meeting up with this vision?

3. Are your goals in line with your husband's goals? Discuss this with him.

4. What changes can and should be made in the next year? Sometimes you need to make some tough choices, such as cutting back on the kids' activities, getting an additional car, hiring something out, getting a second job temporarily or quitting your current one, addressing health issues, and so on.

    - Home

    - Marriage

    - Family as a whole

    - Child #1

    - Child #2

    - Child #3

    - Child #4

    - Schedule

5. What are the steps you are going to take to get there?

    Step 1:

    Step 2:

    Step 3:

    Step 4:

    Step 5:

Day 2—The "Oikodespotein"

"To be queen of a household is a powerful thing." ~ Jill Scott

In Bible times "workers at home" were serious, valued leaders in the family. Being the woman over the household was *not* a light assignment. The home was the place of business, learning, security, and success—the center out of which all of life operated for the family. So, when God called wives to step up and lead in this vital region called "the home," it was, and still is, quite an arduous assignment. Oh, the trust and confidence He must have in us to call us to such a great responsibility!

Would you agree that there are countless ways and areas a wife can place her energies? When coupled with a societal attitude that work at home is thankless, anonymous, and endless drudgery, you can see why women today often choose to spend their energies outside of the home. Yet, home is exactly where a bulk of her time and energy is needed. The leadership and marshaling of resources you bring to your home are essential to the success of your marriage and family. Day Two will introduce the concept of the "oikodespotein" and all that it means. Believe it or not, it's a title women can be proud of.

1. Continue reading on page 106-114 in *God's Radical Plan for Wives*.

Biblical Insight

2. What is the Greek meaning of the two important phrases below? Write the Greek word and meaning for each as recorded in the book.

   "oikourgos" =

   Meaning:

   "oikodespotein" =

   Meaning:

3. Read Titus 2:4-5. What does God call older women to do?

4. What does He call younger women to do? Why?

5. Read 1 Timothy 5:14. What does Paul want the younger widows to do? Why?

6. According to the verses above, how could a wife who doesn't keep her home in order dishonor God or give the enemy an occasion for reproach or rebuke? What is at stake?

Choices, Choices
7. Write if you agree or disagree with the following statement? Why or why not?
   "The home is not the only place where a woman can direct her energy, but it is the number one priority."

8. Can you identify areas in your own life where you spend a large portion of your time and energies outside of the home?

9. Are there any changes in priorities you need to make?

A Call to Wives
10. Is a wife vital to the development of a great marriage and family? Why or why not?

11. What does your role in the domestic area look like? Is it working for you and your family?

12. Are there changes that need to be made, such as delegating, hiring some help, or stepping up more to handle some things yourself? Do you need to relocate your job? Cut back on hours?

Working Wives

13. If you work outside of the home, how do you and your husband handle the domestic arena? Are you a team? Do you share in the duties?

14. If you struggle in this area, what can you do to make both your work life and domestic life more balanced? Think of a few tangible ideas.

Signs and Symptoms of a Needed Change

15. Have you noticed any of the symptoms as described in the reading coming from your husband or other members of your family? What are they?

16. As the house leader, how can you take the initiative to take the needed changes? What changes can you take to bring your home to a place of relational peace and harmony?

Digging Deeper

The Bible talks about several women who successfully managed significant, important work outside the home, while still holding the responsibility of managing her home. Read about one or more of the following women. Write in your journal anything that stands out to you regarding her life, profession, and duties.

17. To dig a little deeper, do a word search on her name in a concordance or on a web-based Bible program such as www.Biblegateway.com.

    ✓ Deborah, a judge (Judges 4)
    ✓ Pricilla, a tentmaker (Acts 18, Romans 16)
    ✓ Lydia, a seller of purple cloth (Acts 16:11-15)

Daily Wrap-Up

In your own words, finish this sentence as it pertains to today's lesson: "If I am to follow *God's Radical Plan for Wives,* I need to work on…."

Think About This!

"The most significant jobs in any culture are those that directly impact the future. This is why there has been an honored place in every nation and culture to the role of the wife and mother."

"A man needs his wife to be the best leader she can possibly be in the domestic arena, even if she also works outside the home."

Marriage Exercise #2

Evaluating Your Resources

Having the right resources (time, energy, and money) are vital to accomplishing the goals of the family and successful management of the home. She who understands the family budget will ultimately be successful in her God-given role as a home manager. Make it a priority within the next month to look at the finances, develop a budget (if you don't already have one), and decide on how things can and should be different. This is an activity best done together as a couple so that you can establish goals together and be on the same page in terms of spending. Keep each other accountable to stay on budget. If your husband is responsible for this area, ask him to walk you through the finances so that you can understand where the household stands. It's good for you to know that.

There are many wonderful tools to help families learn how to manage money more effectively. Check out *Crown Ministries* by Larry Burkett, *Financial Peace University* by Dave Ramsey, or research Ron Blue's Ministry for more information. Consider these questions and answer them to the best of your ability. You may need more time than you have today but don't give up! Revisit this page or create a form on your computer, answering all questions until they are completed. Ultimately, you want to know the following information:

- How much money does the family have this month?

- Where will it be spent?

- Where should it be spent—more of "x" and less of "y"?

- Are there ways to cut costs?

- Is there a way to build a savings account?

- How will we pay for X, Y, Z?

Day 3—The Heart of the Home

The concept of "HOME" is more than just bricks and mortar; more than the physical building we live in. *Smithsonian Magazine* has a great article about the idea of home with this quote: *"Be it ever so humble, it's more than just a place. It's also an idea—one where the heart is."* Here are some other quotes about "home":

"Charity begins at home." (1 Timothy 5:4)

"When the pressures of the world intrude, there is no shelter like a peaceful home."

"Home is where the heart is." – Pliny the Elder

"Home interprets heaven. Home is heaven for beginners." – Charles Henry Parkhurst

A poem by Lena Guilbert Ford ~ *Keep the Home Fires Burning*, 1915

> *Keep the home fires burning,*
> *While your hearts are yearning;*
> *Though your lads are far away*
> *They dream of coming home.*
> *There's a silver lining*
> *Through the dark cloud shining;*
> *Turn the dark cloud inside out,*
> *Till the boys come home.*

The *Heart of the Home* is the very essence of the place where our families come home to every day. As women and wives, we have a tremendous impact on making a home—either a good, beneficial impact or a bad, negative one. As the domestic leader of our homes, we get to shape the very nature of "home" in the hearts and minds of our kids and husbands. Women are the heartbeat. Today you will see that we have a bigger, more important job than we realize. It's awesome how God must really trust us, since he gave us responsibility over so much.

Looking back to the story of Bill and Sally, Sally recognized her error with humility and readily re-established the role she was intended to fill—*the stability and nurturing force of the home.*

1. Look up the following verses and record what God says about the role of a wife in the home.
   Proverbs 14:1

> *Note: In Hebrew, the word "build" used in this verse means to obtain children, make, and repair, to set up. In the dictionary, building something means to "increase or strengthen by adding gradually to; develop or give form to according to a plan or process; create."*

Titus 2:3-5

1 Timothy 5:14

Proverbs 31:27

2. Answer the following statements True (T) or False (F):

   _____ God's desire is for wives to lead and manage their homes. They are just the right person for the job.

   _____ A smooth running home is not necessary to the husband, family, and ultimately the larger society. It doesn't really matter in the big scheme of things.

   _____ God commanded wives to manage the home because it is more fun and easier for them to do.

   _____ Women are uniquely gifted to manage the activities in the home that result in a stable marriage and family.

   _____ Just like other leaders in leadership roles, delegating tasks at home is encouraged and key to managing the home successfully.

3. It takes a special kind of person with special skills to manage and lead a household. God doesn't want women to cheapen the job He has given us. Instead, He wants us to recognize that taking care of matters at home is part of His plan for stability in the family. Place a check in the boxes below that describe the unique skills, abilities, and attitudes that are required to manage and lead a home successfully:

   - ☐ Resourcefulness
   - ☐ Idleness
   - ☐ Being insightful
   - ☐ Knowledgeable
   - ☐ Selfishness
   - ☐ Preparation/Planning
   - ☐ Being wasteful
   - ☐ A willingness to learn
   - ☐ Resolve
   - ☐ Ability to multi-task
   - ☐ Laziness
   - ☐ Helpful attitude
   - ☐ Intuition
   - ☐ Organizational skills
   - ☐ Money sense
   - ☐ Disorganized
   - ☐ A sense of purpose
   - ☐ Attentive to details
   - ☐ Stubborn spirit
   - ☐ Efficiency

4. Looking at the descriptive words above, do any of these attributes describe you? It's important to acknowledge both the positive attributes you possess, while also being aware of areas that need to be changed or worked on. Record five positive traits you do well and five negative ones to be work on.

Positive Traits	Negative Traits
1.	1.
2.	2.
3.	3.
4.	4.
5.	5.

Daily Wrap-Up

In your own words, finish this sentence as it pertains to today's lesson: "If I am to follow *God's Radical Plan for Wives,* I need to work on…."

Think About This!

"God directs wives to care for the home because she has the unique skills that provide for a stable marriage and family."

"The Word of God will gain added value in the eyes of society when the ability to lead domestically is put into practice by godly wives."

Marriage Exercise #3

Training the Children

Successful parents spend time and energy training the children to be self-controlled and well behaved in social situations and at home. While it is difficult and requires patience, diligence, and perseverance, it is well worth it. Consider the following questions for each child in the household:

1. Which negative and positive training methods need to be used with your children?
   - Verbal reprimand
   - Repetition
   - Work
   - Exercises
   - Rewards
   - Isolation
   - Restraint
   - Chastisement
   - Removal of privileges

2. How do you expect your child to act in these situations? What can you do to train them accordingly?
   - At restaurants
   - At relatives' homes
   - At parties
   - At church
   - At home
   - In their rooms

3. Who do you need to recruit, employ, or expose your child to in order to give them the highest possible chance for their character, ethics, skills, grades, talents, and salvation to be assured?

4. In ten years, your child will be successful if… How can you make sure those things happen?

Day 4—The Wisdom To Build Her Home

1. Today's reading includes pages 115-122 in *God's Radical Plan for Wives*.

Risks of Ignoring the Role

2. What are some risks of not taking domestic leadership seriously?

3. Why is the wife's involvement with the children, home, and peace at home so vital to a husband?

Male and Female Differences

4. How do men and women typically view home and family differently?

5. Are there differences in the way you and your husband view home and family?

6. In your Bible, read Proverbs 31:10-31. Reflect on the attitude and intentions of the "Noble Wife" described in the verses. Write any notes about her in your journal or on the spaces below.

7. Look up the meanings of the following words that may describe this woman of excellence.

   Wisdom:

   Prudent:

   Sensible:

   Shrewd:

   Discerning:

8. Considering the meanings of the words above, write a paragraph summarizing what a wife who exercises "wisdom" might be like:

Daily Wrap-Up

In your own words, finish this sentence as it pertains to today's lesson: "If I am to follow *God's Radical Plan for Wives,* I need to work on...."

> **Think About This!**
>
> "If a wife abdicates her leadership responsibility, she diminishes the drawing power of her love to bring her husband to her and his ability to reach his highest potential."
>
> "Remember that men need to be engaged and active in the household. Make space for his involvement."

Day 5—Developing a Plan

1. Read pages 123-129 in *God's Radical Plan for Wives*.

Danger of Too Much Domestic Leadership
2. What role should husbands play in the home? Does he have a role?
   See Marriage Exercise #5.

3. Do you involve your husband in planning and problem-solving regarding the home? If so, how has this benefited the household? If not, why?

Developing a Plan
4. Below is a list of categories for maintaining and managing a home. Consider each category and do the following, writing your responses on the lines below:
   a. Identify your *strengths* (S) and *weaknesses* (W) for each.
   b. Record action steps to overcome the weak areas, such as delegating, hiring out, learning a skill, or _____ (be creative).
   c. Determine what family member or other resource you might be able to recruit, train, and manage to help you in this area (Husband, Child #1, #2, #3).

   (Note: Perfection is not the goal in any of these areas. Sometimes we need to pick our battles and give ourselves a little grace.)

   Clothing Maintenance:

   S:

   W:

   Action Steps:
   1.
   2.

   Who can help me?

Food Storage/Preparation:

S:
W:

Action Steps:
1.
2.

Who can help me?

House Cleaning/Maintenance/Repairs:

S:

W:

Action Steps:
1.
2.

Who can help me?

Yard Maintenance/Repairs/Gardening:

S:

W:

Action Steps:
1.
2.

Who can help me?

Beautifying Inside and Outside:

S:

W:

Action Steps:
1.
2.

Who can help me?

Budget Management/Finances:

S:

W:

Action Steps:
1.
2.

Who can help me?

Technology Upkeep:

S:

W:

Action Steps:
1.
2.

Who can help me?

Children's Schooling/Activities Management:

S:

W:

Action Steps:
1.
2.

Who can help me?

Children's Moral Development/Discipline:

S:

W:

Action Steps:
1.
2.

Who can help me?

Giving/Serving:

S:

W:

Action Steps:
1.
2.

Who can help me?

Pets/Animals:

S:

W:

Action Steps:
1.
2.

Who can help me?

Marriage Exercise #4

Home Maintenance

1. What would your home life be like if you accomplished the most important projects, clean ups, and maintenance in the next year? List five things in order of priority:

    -
    -
    -
    -
    -

2. Whom do you have to recruit, hire, or invite over to move the home to a level of an acceptable, even pleasant, dwelling place?

Marriage Exercise #5

Valuing and Incorporating His Ideas

A man may decide to opt out of involvement with his marriage and family if it is clear that his ideas, plans, and his presence do not make him a major player at home. The following questions are meant to get at the root of why husbands might not be interested in engaging in home and family.

1. What would your house look like if your husband had complete say on how it was decorated? Do any of his ideas or thoughts show up in how your home looks?

2. What would be different if your husband had complete control over spending? Do you implement any of his ideas on saving or spending?

3. What would be different about the children if his plans for clothing, behavior, schooling, and discipline were implemented fully? Are there any particular areas that bother or annoy him that you can help with?

4. How different would your schedule be if your husband were completely in charge of it? What aspects of your schedule reflect his ideas, wishes, or desires?

5. If your husband could pick your friends, would anything change? Would anything change in your social life either independently or as a couple if your husband had his way?

Weekly Wrap Up
In your own words, finish this sentence as it pertains to this week's lessons: "If I am to follow *God's Radical Plan for Wives,* I need to work on...."

Day 1:

Day 2:

Day 3:

Day 4:

Day 5:

What is the **#1 take-a-way** you had from this week's lesson?

A Prayer for Our Home...

Father, I am grateful for the man you've given me in this marriage, and I want him to always come back to me. Please help me to meet this need for peace in the home. May it always be a place of refuge, warmth, and love. Help us to work together to manage our household by communicating and delegating, each of us working together in our best way. Help me to lovingly guide him in what I need from him to make everything work. May the work of my hands at home and outside of the home be a blessing to my family.
In Jesus' Name,
Amen

Lesson 5

Chapter 6—Intimacy

Lesson 5

Chapter 6—Intimacy

His Loudest Need

Everyone has a need for intimacy to a certain degree, but there are many factors to consider when addressing it—are we male or female, young or old, healthy or ill, stressed or relaxed, are there young children at home? Women and men typically have very different needs in this area. Men generally need sexual release to fill a physiological need, but they also have an emotional and spiritual component filled by physical intimacy. While sex is important for some women more than others, the physiological needs are typically less demanding than a man's; and women are somewhat able to fulfill the emotional need for intimacy in non-sexual ways through friendships and so on.

Our need for physical intimacy often depends on our ages and stages in life and what we have going on. Many older couples I have talked to about this subject agree that as you get older, the need for sexual intercourse changes; intimacy is achieved in other ways. I know from experience that couples with young children struggle in finding time and energy to be together, let alone to be intimate. In those cases, intimacy is achieved by extending grace and in sharing the struggle together.

For the purposes of this study, we will address this physiological and emotional need for intimacy in husbands. We'll see how once this need is met, it opens up a gateway for getting our needs met. Of all the needs in men, there is perhaps none greater (or louder) than the need for sexual intimacy. As women, we really should empathize for our men. Imagine having a need that is constantly there, building in intensity and strength. Once it's finally met, it begins again after a short time of contentment. At the strongest point, it's all they can focus on—"get that need met!"

As a woman, I can't identify with a need that is that loud or strong except for maybe intense hunger pains or physical pain. But I can meet those needs myself by eating or taking medicine. In talking to men about their need for sex, they describe it like an itch. It starts out small but the longer time goes by without it being scratched, the prickling, itching, and pressure become so intense it consumes every thought, idea, motivation, and desire. In other words, the entire focus IS the itch. He can't think. Sleeping becomes an issue as he tosses and turns. He loses his edge at work because he can't concentrate. He becomes grouchy, irritable, and impatient around you and the children. Worse, he starts to notice every female in the area or pictures or shapes of anything that look remotely like breasts. In general, he is so distracted that he is not able to be the man God calls him to be. And sometimes he falls into temptation by doing unrighteous things that leave him feeling guilty, ashamed, or frustrated.

This is where you come in. Remember from chapter five that you were created by God to be his "help mate." You are the one that God gave him to help him fulfill his righteous potential. Learning to meet this need in your husband is crucial to his success in every area of his life. This week's homework is going to challenge you to look at some intimate details between you and your man. My hope is that you won't be embarrassed or shy. Instead, treat this as an opportunity to be reflective, interested, and even experimental. At the very least, maybe you'll gain an understanding of where he's coming from, what he experiences daily, and what he needs from you.

Day 1—Understanding Our Differences

1. Read pages 131-141 in *God's Radical Plan for Wives*.

2. In your dictionary, look up the meaning of the word *intimacy* regarding relationships and record its meaning and synonyms.

Scriptural Explanation
In your Bible, look up the following scriptures and answer the questions.

3. **1 Corinthians 7:1-5**
   What do the verses say about sexual relations between a man and a wife?

   What does this passage tell the man to do regarding his wife?

   What does the passage tell the woman to do regarding her husband?

   Verse 5 says that husbands and wives are not to deprive each other from sex except in times of agreed-upon abstinence for prayer. What reason does it give for not depriving one another?

   What could either of you be tempted to do? What are potential dangers to your marriage if this scripture is not taken seriously?

4. **Genesis 2:24, Matthew 19:4-6**
   What do you think this verse is saying about God's design for intimacy between a man and his wife?

   Record any insights you gained from these verses.

   God designed marriage to be an intimate connection between a man and a woman, so that a couple can be all God wants them to be. Do you see? As a couple, you are God-ordained to belong to each other. You are his and he is yours!

5. God hardwired men and women differently in this area of intimacy. From your reading, describe the differences between men and women.
   Kinds of Contact
   Men:

   Women:

   How the Need is Met
   Men:

   Women:

   Physiological Considerations
   Men:

   Women:

   Emotional Considerations
   Men:

   Women:

113

Struggles
Men:

Women:

6. From your reading, answer the following statements True (T) or False (F):

   _____ Sexual intimacy is just about satisfying physical or sexual feelings.

   _____ A wife can help protect her husband from the temptations of anonymous sex and pornography by understanding his sexual cycle and doing her best to meet his need.

   _____ When a wife consistently and lovingly meets her husband's sexual needs, he loves the body she currently has and sees it as God's gift to him.

   _____ There are no risks involved in not meeting the sexual needs in husbands.

   _____ God's mystery of intimacy lies in the fact that a man finds his wife even more beautiful and attractive as she grows older.

   _____ The only kind of sex that is meaningful is "WOW" sex.

Understanding Types of Sexual Intimacy

7. Name the three types of intimacy and the purpose for each. How do you and your husband relate in each of these areas. Could there be improvements in any of these areas?

Risks of Not Meeting the Need

8. Are there risks of not meeting the sexual need in your husband? What are some of them?

9. Have you witnessed any of these risks firsthand in your own marriage? How did you react?

Sexual Self-Image

10. In what ways does your own self-image affect sexual intimacy with your husband?

A Prayer For Us...

*Dear Lord, You have made us to be united in love together physically, emotionally, mentally, and spiritually. What an awesome gift you have given us to experience each other's bodies and find pleasure in them! For whatever reason, though, you have created us differently and with different needs. Help me, Lord, as his wife, to meet that need that is so loud and deep within him. Give me empathy to his plight and struggle. Make me in tune with his needs and then give me the energy, attitude, and desire to fill it. It's truly a gift you've given us. May I never forget that.
In Jesus' Name,
Amen*

Daily Wrap-Up

In your own words, finish this sentence as it pertains to today's lesson: "If I am to follow *God's Radical Plan for Wives,* I need to work on...."

Think About This!

"If a wife waits until she felt like having sexual relations, she would not be meeting her husband's need in this area." (From *Every Man's Battle*, by Stephen Arterburn)

"If home is the place where this relentless need is lovingly and tenderly met in his life, he will be more open to the wisdom, correction, and development his wife can offer him."

Marriage Exercise #1

Become the Initiator

Try this!

When you know about a potential stressful situation that will require cooperation between you and your husband, initiate intimacy with him beforehand. You'll be surprised at how much better you work together and how much less tension there is between you. This could include, but is not limited to:

The night before a big vacation or fast-paced trip.

The day or night before a visit from out-of-town guests – like your parents or in-laws.

At the beginning of major renovations (and during, too).

The day before a business trip for either of you.

The day or night before an important meeting for work.

The day or night before you are due to receive some important news.

Day 2—Loving First as a Godly Wife Strategy

The secret to keeping your husband coming to you to meet his sexual needs, rather than an outside source, is dependent upon you as his wife. Loving him first is a godly wife strategy that works. The wise woman realizes that when she meets his deepest needs, she then has an opportunity to train her husband how to meet her deepest needs. He will keep coming to her to have his needs met if she is always there for him. Then she can wisely orient him to her needs through her strong, consistent love for him.

1. Continue reading on pages 141-150 in *God's Radical Plan for Wives*.

Loving First as a Godly Wife Strategy
2. In your Bible, look up 1 John 4:19 and record what it says.

   Does this verse apply to husbands and wives? How can wives demonstrate love for her husband in the area of sexual intimacy?

3. The difference you'll make in loving him first will be wonderful. Look up the verses below and write down anything that might help you apply this principle.

   Ephesians 4:1-3

   Ephesians 5:1-2

   1 Corinthians 13:7

   1 Corinthians 16:14

   Galatians 5:13

Are you the one with the unmet sexual need?
If you struggle in the area of meeting your husband's sexual need, you're not alone. On average, 54% of men think about sex every day, compared to only 19% of wives.[2] Women just don't tend to need it or even think about it as much as they. So what can you do? Psalm 54:4 says, "Behold, God is my helper; the Lord is the upholder of my life." This verse is there to remind you that God is your helper in all things.

If you don't feel able to meet your husband's need at the moment but you know in your heart he needs you to, pray for God to help you find the right attitude, the right mood, an increase in desire, and to help you put aside your stress or anxiety. Watch and see. He will do it! Loving your husband in this way is directly at the center of His will, so your prayers will be heard and answered. When you seek God's will and help in this area, He will give you the strength, insight, and wisdom you need to meet your husband's needs on an on-going basis.

There are other women where the opposite is true. Maybe you are more interested in sexual intimacy than your husband is and you don't understand why? If this is your experience, Psalm 139:14 assures you that you are fearfully and wonderfully made. There is nothing wrong with you—you are beautiful! Seek to understand what is going on with your husband. It could come down to a number of issues, including the ones listed in the reading. Hang in there, don't give up!

4. Below are key points from the reading. Put a check next to the ones that were new thoughts to you:

- [ ] The only person in the whole world who can meet your husband's sexual need without guilt is you, his wife.

- [ ] Just as a woman is not drawn to her husband unless he gives her honor, understanding, and affection, a man is not drawn to his wife if she is not meeting his number one need.

- [ ] God will help you meet your husband's needs when you make the choice to surrender to your spouse by filling him up with your love.

- [ ] Meeting the physical needs of your husband can be effective in accomplishing your needs or the needs of the family.

- [ ] A man has a deep and lasting need for sexual intimacy, and he will adjust and grow and change in order to keep this need met.

- [ ] Even if a woman doesn't feel like it, she is still called to meet this need in her man.

---

[2] Cutrer, William, M.D., Glahn, Sandra, *Sexual Intimacy in Marriage*. (Grand Rapids: Kregel Publishing, 2007), 87.

Signs and Symptoms of His Need

Look at the descriptions in the Marriage Exercise #1 in *God's Radical Plan for Wives* that talk about the signs and symptoms your husband displays when he needs an intimate encounter with you. For example: more touching, find him staring at you, compliments you more, and so on. Other clues include an increased interest in women in general, irritability, and sleeplessness.

5. What signs does your husband give you to let you know he is interested?

Determine His Sexual Cycle

6. Starting right after intimacy, how long does it take before these symptoms appear again? *(Check one)*

    Every...   Day   _____
              Other Day   _____
              Third Day   _____
              Fourth Day   _____
              Fifth Day   _____
              Sixth Day   _____
              Seventh Day   _____
              Twice a Month   _____
              Once a Month   _____

    Note: A man will often have a backlogged interest in sexual intimacy that may not allow you to read it correctly at first. If it has been a while, you may have to initiate sex more frequently for a week or two in order to get a correct reading. Once you understand his cycle, figure out a way to keep track of it. Consider writing it on your calendar. That way, if you know the day is coming, your mind and body will more likely be prepared for your sexual encounter.

Daily Wrap-Up

In your own words, finish this sentence as it pertains to today's lesson: "If I am to follow *God's Radical Plan for Wives,* I need to work on...."

Think About This!

"They need it, so we do it."

"When one side of what is supposed to be a mutual relationship is consistently under-loved, it puts a strain on the relationship."

Day 3—Meeting His Sexual Need

In most marriages, meeting the sexual need of husbands is the number one challenge for wives. Yet we now know it is vital to him as a relational need. Understanding his point of view will go a long way toward bringing harmony and balance to the marriage. Not only will his need be met in this area, but it can provide leverage for wives to suggest, direct, and encourage the fulfillment of her needs with a much greater level of success. It is a great mystery how this works, but it is true.

This looks a lot different to older couples or those experiencing illness. The need for intimacy is still important, even if it can't be expressed sexually. Making time for each other, non-sexual physical touch, and communication helps to maintain a good relationship.

1. Continue reading on pages 150-156 in *God's Radical Plan for Wives*.

Meeting this Need in Everyday Life

2. Write your response to the following passage from the reading. What does this look like in your marriage?

    "Since it is a reoccurring event and it involves a person of high priority, it is something that takes priority over other action items to see that it gets done. She does not wait until the mood strikes her, or when she feels like it."

3. How does your life stage affect intimacy and sexual expression? Older couples? Young children? Illness?

Planning Your Sexual Encounter

Spontaneity is wonderful but not always possible or necessary. We must resist the idea that planning for sex will reduce the "romantic value." A highly impactful and motivating way to demonstrate your love for your husband is to spend time thinking of ways to meet his needs sexually. It is important to know that men love variety in places, times, positions, use of props, and so on. As his wife, your planning, creativity, understanding, and initiation in this area will be received with unquestionable excitement and gratitude. Answer the following questions to the best of your abilities. If possible, find a way to ask your husband what he thinks so you'll know for sure.

4. When (how often) will he need sex this week? What day(s) this week? Time-of-day?

5. How will you meet his need for sexual intimacy this week? Work this out in your schedule.

6. How much time will you be able to put aside to meet his need this week?

7. What preparations need to be made to ensure a positive experience? Consider physical grooming, props, and arrangements for the children.

Long-Term Planning: Schedule Time Away
Many wives as not as relaxed at home as they would like to be for their husband. Scheduling weekends away from the kids, the pets, house, and chores is crucial to successful marriages.
Note: If you are worried about leaving your kids, please trust me when I say that time away is good for them and good for you. It comes down to the priority of the relationships. A good marriage does a happy family make!

8. In the next six months, when can you arrange for a weekend away or an off-site "rendezvous"? When would be a good time to go? Describe where you would like to go and how you would like to spend the time. Don't forget to consider your budget!

9. Who can take care of the kids and pets for you? Relatives? Is there an opportunity to trade with good friends?

Educating Your Husband
Our culture can give men and women a skewed understanding of what is pleasing sexually to the other. Educating your husband about what is pleasing to you is advantageous to both of you. It's not always easy, but it is important.

10. List three things you would like your husband to DO to <u>help you warm up</u> before a sexual encounter. Examples could be helping to get the kids put to bed, doing the dishes, letting you relax a bit at night, physical touching or snuggling. Now write down three things you would like him to STOP DOING, such as pouting, nagging, not helping, and so on.

DO	**STOP DOING**
1)	1)
2)	2)
3)	3)

11. What are three things you would like your husband to ADD to your sexual encounters that <u>you would enjoy</u>? What are three things you would like him to STOP DOING that <u>is not enjoyable</u>? Consider the five senses: sight, touch, smell, taste, and sound to get you started.

ADD	**STOP DOING**
1)	1)
2)	2)
3)	3)

12. What are three things you would like your husband to DO <u>after</u> a sexual encounter? What are three things you like him to NOT DO <u>after</u> a sexual encounter?

DO	**DON'T DO**
1)	1)
2)	2)
3)	3)

13. What are three things you don't know about sexual intimacy but would like to know about? Commit to finding the answers either from a trusted friend or an intimacy book for married couples.

1)

2)

3)

14. When is your husband most likely able to receive new information in the sexual arena? List the four ways.

    -

    -

    -

    -

Daily Wrap-Up

In your own words, finish this sentence as it pertains to today's lesson: "If I am to follow *God's Radical Plan for Wives,* I need to work on…."

Marriage Exercise #2

The Three-Day Challenge

Want to shake things up? Make a point to meet his need sexually every **third day** for the next two weeks. Do this without his knowing what you are up to and then observe any changes that develop in your husband. If your husband's sexual cycle is less than three days, then adjust this challenge accordingly.

Day 4—Problems with Sexual Intimacy and Boundaries

1. Today's reading includes pages 156-161 in *God's Radical Plan for Wives.*

2. God intends for you and your husband to enjoy sexual intimacy that is beautiful and fulfilling for both of you, yet is God-honoring. That means that the marriage bed is considered to be "holy ground" and great care should be taken to protect and preserve it. Let's look up the following verses and record what it says.
Hebrews 13:4

    Ephesians 5:3

3. Look up the following words in your dictionary:

    Purity/Impurity

    Moral/Immoral

    Pervert

4. Look up 1 Corinthians 6:12-20 in your Bible. These verses, written by Paul, talk about sexual immorality. Write down the key points of each verse in the spaces below:

    Verse 12:

    Verse 13:

    Verse 15:

Verse 16:

Verse 17:

Verse 18:

Verse 19:

Verse 20:

Summarize what this passage is saying? How does is relate to your marriage?

Common Intimacy Problems
There are some common intimacy problems that, unfortunately, do occur. Some have darker forces at play.
5. From your reading, write down any areas of concern you have for your marriage and some possible solutions.

Boundaries to Intimacy
A wife needs to know that even though one of her main roles is to fulfill the sexual need in her husband, by no means does this mean doing so under violent or harsh circumstances.

6. What type of boundaries should a godly woman set for herself?

7. There are all kinds of sexual perversions that destroy a person's self-worth. Sexual fulfillment should never involve these practices. Looking at Marriage Exercise #6 in *God's Radical Plan for Wives,* consider actions that would be considered "unholy" in your marriage bed. Communicate with your husband about the things you are uncomfortable with.

Addressing Unfaithfulness

8. In your Bible, look up Matthew 5:27-28. Record it in the spaces below:

9. According to the passage, would viewing pornography be considered marital unfaithfulness or not? Why or why not?

10. How do you think this pertains to the use of pornography, either separately or within the marriage? Bring any concerns you have about this area to God in prayer and, if possible, seek out godly wisdom from a pastor or mentor.

11. How can you help your husband refrain from what is described in Matthew 5:27-28? Put a check next to any that apply. *Please keep in mind that you are not responsible for another person's sin. But putting these practices into play may help him have the energy he needs to overcome temptations.*

    ☐ Understand his sexual cycle
    ☐ Add variety and spice to your love life
    ☐ Meet his need consistently
    ☐ Initiate
    ☐ Make plans for time away with just him
    ☐ Touch him throughout the day
    ☐ Groom and take care of yourself
    ☐ Be spontaneous and creative
    ☐ Make time for him
    ☐ Meet the three-day challenge (or less)
    ☐ Communicate your likes and dislikes, do's and don'ts

Closing Remarks

If you suspect that your husband is engaged in pornography in any way, shape or form, it is critical to the health of your marriage to help him overcome this problem before it becomes an addiction. Get help quickly by getting educated. Consider counseling, talking to a pastor, or purchasing other resources—perhaps a combination of all three. Some great books on this subject include *An Affair of the Mind* by Laurie Hall, *Every Man's Battle* by Stephen Arteburn, and *Mission Possible: Winning the Battle Over Temptation* by Gil Stieglitz. Reading these yourself and having your husband read them too will lead to a deeper understanding of the horrible effects of pornography. It's something to be taken very seriously.

Daily Wrap-Up

In your own words, finish this sentence as it pertains to today's lesson: "If I am to follow *God's Radical Plan for Wives,* I need to work on...."

Think About This!

"A faithful, supportive wife is crucial to a man as he works through the issues that may be at the root of his problems."

"Make every attempt to keep the marriage bed 'holy.' God is merciful and forgiving when we confess our sins to him."

Day 5—Four Intimate Ways That Show Him Love

Not only do men need their wives to meet their need sexually, they need them to be active participants. It isn't enough to just offer up your body so he can take care of his need. No! Today we'll learn about four basic things men need from their wives intimately.

1. Conclude the reading with pages 161-169 in *God's Radical Plan for Wives*.

2. List the four ways that show him you love him intimately.

    -

    -

    -

    -

3. From your reading, answer the following statements True (T) or False (F):

    _____ Your husband couldn't care less if you want to be involved in sexual intercourse with him or not. As long as his need is met, he's happy.

    _____ One way to show your husband you really love him is to initiate sex.

    _____ A man believes that if his wife never initiates sex, there is something wrong with him.

    _____ Men don't mind if the woman isn't enjoying herself.

    _____ A man tends to rate himself as a husband on his ability to satisfy his wife sexually.

    _____ Men develop incredible tension sexually and are just as happy to release it themselves.

    _____ Our men need us to have an attitude that says, "I'm giving you my best."

    _____ Men express their emotions and feelings through intimate encounters with their wife.

    _____ A wise wife realizes he has something to say through how he has sex.

    _____ A woman should never worry about her husband going outside of the marriage to have his sexual needs met.

Initiating Intimacy
Consider the following questions regarding how you should initiate intimacy.

4. Think of a time when you initiated sexual interest and fulfillment. Was it positive or negative? How did he respond?

5. Below are ways that could demonstrate sexual interest to your husband. Check the ones that would most appeal to your husband. Which ones are you willing to try?
   - _____ feigning disinterest
   - _____ dressing up, down, or "sexy"
   - _____ unusual attire, costumes
   - _____ flirting
   - _____ verbal hints
   - _____ sexual stare
   - _____ spoken requests
   - _____ personal touch
   - _____ sensual kiss
   - _____ verbal scenarios
   - _____ undressing

Signaling Intimacy
It can be much more fun to have a secret signal between you and your spouse for intimacy. Some couples fall into a rut, leading to a rather bland sex life. In fact, sometimes the way a spouse signals for sex can even be a mood killer!

6. Write about your own examples used in your marriage. What works best for the two of you?

   Direct Request

   Indirect Request

   Verbal Signal

   Tangible Signal

A Prayer For Our Home...

Lord, I pray for protection for our marriage. Please help my husband and me to keep any darkness from our home by maintaining our intimacy. Help us to understand any areas where we are weak or areas that maybe aren't holy or pleasing to you that need adjustment. Keep my husband strong in his resolve to remain true to our marriage—keep his eyes focused only on me. Keep my attention focused on him to meet his needs.
In Jesus' Name,
Amen

Daily Wrap-Up

In your own words, finish this sentence as it pertains to today's lesson: "If I am to follow *God's Radical Plan for Wives,* I need to work on...."

Think About This!

"When a wife initiates sex before his cycle reaches its peak, she demonstrates that she understands him and cares for him."

"A man can tend to think, *'Since she doesn't want me as her lover, she doesn't really love me.'*"

Weekly Wrap Up

In your own words, finish this sentence as it pertains to this week's lessons: "If I am to follow *God's Radical Plan for Wives,* I need to work on...."

Day 1:

Day 2:

Day 3:

Day 4:

Day 5:

What is the **#1 take-a-way** you had from this week's lesson?

Lesson 6

Chapter 7: Companionship

Lesson 6

Chapter 7—Companionship

Loving Him As A Friend

Men and women have very different friendship needs. Women tend to be more social and able to form friendships easily with other women. For some, this is vital to her balance and happiness in life. I, for one, crave good old-fashioned girl time now and then. I love a good coffee date or chatting over lunch with a good friend or two. We swap stories about motherhood, our dreams, ideas, and our struggles in life. There is something wonderful about getting to know other women and being involved in their lives. A pattern set from ancient times, women gathered at the local well collecting both water and encouragement for the day. Our need for companionship was valuable then, and it is just as valuable to us today.

Men have different companionship needs. If they do have friends, they are usually guys they work with or share a common recreational interest. Since they don't typically have a lot of close day-to-day friendships, they rely on their wives to fill that need. You might say we are their built-in companions and, if you think about it, that's a good thing! While a woman may really love spending time with her girlfriends, she needs to also understand companionship love and the part she plays in her husband's life. In this week's lesson, we will learn more about this need in men and how best to meet it.

Day 1—A "Side-By-Side" Love

1. Read pages 171-179 in *God's Radical Plan for Wives*.

2. Reviewing the story of Kelly and Steve, answer the following questions:

   What was the key problem with Kelly and Steve's relationship?

   What do you think about Kelly's response? Do you agree that she handled the situation correctly or not?

3. Why do men like the recreational pursuits they do? What do they fulfill in him?

Scriptural Explanation

4. What are two things a man gains from his companions?

   -

   -

5. God addresses this companionship need that men have in Titus 2:3-5. The word "*love*" in verse 4 is the Greek word *phileo* meaning brotherly love – a friendship or companionship love. What is it that God wants wives to do?

6. Why is being a good companion for your husband important to understand? What will you not have access to unless you meet this need?

Risks of Not Meeting the Companionship Need

7. There are *three main risks* that wives take when she doesn't meet this companionship need in her husband. What are they?

   -

   -

   -

How to Access His Soul

8. Is this type of love something intuitive for women, or is it something to be *learned*? How do we know?

9. What do the phrases "shoulder-to-shoulder" or "side by side" mean about loving someone?

10. In your dictionary, look up the meaning of the following words as they pertain to marital relationships:

    Companion:

    (Synonym - Accompany):

    Soul mate:

    Fellowship:

    Friend:

11. Describe how you have put this type of "companionship love" into practice in your marriage. Does it come easy to you or is it something you have to work on? What will you do to minimize any risks with your husband? What changes will you make moving forward?

Closing Remarks

In order to minister to your husband's deepest needs, think through the various ways you can be a better companion in the activities that he is passionate about. I realize that this can sometimes seem very "sacrificial" on our part, but remember that you are trying to foster a "friendship" love—*side-by-side* and *shoulder-to-shoulder*. Once you do this, you'll have the benefit of accessing his soul and an exceptional marriage. Your sacrifice will be worthwhile in the end.

Daily Wrap-Up:

In your own words, finish this sentence as it pertains to today's lesson: "If I am to follow *God's Radical Plan for Wives,* I need to work on…."

Think About This!

"The doorway to a man's soul is first through companionship and then active, detached listening."

"If you want a great marriage, becoming a companion to your husband is mandatory."

"The wise woman learns how to enjoy her husband's recreational or passionate pursuits, for it is that woman who is accepted into his soul."

Marriage Exercise #1

Activity Check

1. What activities is your husband thinking about all the time? *(Hint: These are the areas he wants and needs you to be his companion.)*

    Activity #1:

    Activity #2:

    Activity #3:

    Activity #4:

2. The top three worlds men want to share with their wives are usually work, hobbies, and friends. How does your husband like sharing these with you?

    Work:

    Hobbies:

    Friends:

Day 2—The Basics of Friendship: Part I

1. Continue reading pages 179-182 in *God's Radical Plan for Wives*.

2. The Bible says a lot about friendships – like what makes a good friend, the purpose of a friend, and what can separate them. In your Bible, look up and record the following verses.

    Proverbs 17:9

    Proverbs 17:17a

    Proverbs 18:24

    Proverbs 27:6

    Proverbs 27:9

3. Considering the verses above, what things should you do in order to maintain a good *friendship* with your husband?

4. What things should you NOT do to maintain a good *friendship* with your husband?

Six Basic Insights into Friendship (part 1)

5. Write out and provide a basic description of the <u>first three points</u> of understanding friendship:

    - *Friendship begins with...*

    - *Friendship depends upon...*

    - *Friendship deepens when...*

Sharing Basic Information

At one time, you and your husband probably shared your feelings about the nine basic relationships of life.

6. Next to each category, record what you believe your husband understands about each of them at the present time. If you aren't sure, make a point to find out. It can make for some quality discussion time.

   a. God:
      Has his understanding of God changed since you first met your husband?
      Yes _____ No _____
      If *yes,* describe how (i.e., has he grown spiritually, spiritual head of the household, etc.?):

   b. Self:
      Has his viewpoint toward himself changed since you first met your husband?
      Yes ____ No ____
      If *yes,* describe how (i.e., Is he more secure, confident? Where is his focus—on self or others? Does he take time for himself?):

   c. Marriage:
      Has your relationship changed since you first met your husband?
      Yes ____ No _____
      If *yes,* describe how (i.e., Is he still committed? More or less so?):

   d. Family:
      Has your family grown? Yes _____ No _____
      If *yes,* describe how (i.e., How has this affected him? Does he take his role as a father seriously?):

e. Work:
Has his career changed since you first met your husband? Yes _____ No _____
If *yes,* describe how (i.e., How has his attitude toward work changed? How important to him is it? Career changes?):

f. Money:
Has his view of the financial picture changed since you first met your husband?
Yes _____ No _____
If *yes,* describe how (i.e., How does he view money? How important to him is it? What are his worries?):

g. Friends:
Has his need for friendships changed since you first met your husband?
Yes _____ No _____
If *yes,* describe how (i.e., Does he value the same friends? Different friends? Couple friends?)

Sharing Things in Common
Spend time thinking about the activities or interests you and your husband have in common.

7. What do you like to do together? Do you like a common sports team? Discussing politics? Playing with the kids? For more ideas, see page 178-179. Write down any interests you have in common with your husband.

Sharing a Common Perspective

8. Having common perspectives in life is definitely helpful to foster a good friendship. Review the following categories with your husband. Where do you both agree? Where do you disagree? Are there some topics that are off-limits?

Areas:	Agree	Disagree	Viewpoints:
God			His: Hers:
Self			His: Hers:
Marriage			His: Hers:
Family			His: Hers:
Work			His: Hers:
Money			His: Hers:
Friends			His: Hers:

Closing Remarks

Good work today! It's not easy being a good friend all of the time, but it's important to work diligently toward good companionship. Keep in mind that he should be your most valued and treasured friend above all others. If your marriage is strong, he will be there through the good times and the bad times (according to the vows he took when he married you). There are no other friends or even relatives who made those commitments to you. The goal is to foster a strong friendship built on trust, mutual care, and concern for the other spouse by developing common interests and activities to share.

Daily Wrap-Up:

In your own words, finish this sentence as it pertains to today's lesson: "If I am to follow *God's Radical Plan for Wives*, I need to work on...."

Think About This!

"One of the main reasons a man gets married is for companionship."

"Friendship can hit a wall at any time if either side stops sharing basic information with the other one."

"A man reveals some of who he is in the things he likes to do."

Day 3—The Basics of Friendship: Part II

1. Today's reading includes pages 182-185 in *God's Radical Plan for Wives*.

Six Basic Insights into Friendship (part 2)

2. Write out the next three points about maturing friendships and provide a basic description of each.

   Friendship expands when...

   Friendship matures with...

   Friendship is cemented when...

Sharing Common Struggles

3. In your Bible, look up and record the following verses regarding trials and struggle:

   James 1:12

   Romans 5:3-5

4. What blessings do you think come from trials and struggle?

5. What do trials and struggle bring about?

145

6. Think about a struggle you have gone through together as a couple and the effect it has had on your marriage. Did you come through it stronger? Do you still struggle?

Reviewing Common Memories
Reminiscing over shared memories of trips, events, fun activities, or even hard times from which you emerged victorious together can be very healing. In fact, this can be one of the most comforting things for a couple to do. Consider the following questions as they pertain to your marriage and answer accordingly. If preferable, you may write the answers in your journal.

7. Can you describe the time when you and your husband met? What was going on at the time? Where were you in your life? Was it awkward, natural, love-at-first sight, or a gradual building of friendship to love? Consider re-reading journal entries or love letters you shared.

8. Write down a few memories about your wedding. What were the days like leading up to the wedding? What about the morning of your wedding day—do you remember the feeling you had when your eyes popped open? How about the moment when your eyes met his as you walked down the aisle? Do you remember listening to the vow he made to you? What about your first kiss as man and wife?

9. Do you remember your first days as man and wife? The honeymoon? Returning to your new home as a married couple? Look at some pictures of these milestones in your life.

10. Write down a few memories of things you did during your first year of marriage? Did you take any special trips? What were your first jobs? Where was your first home? Who were the special couple friends you had, or what about a memorable night out together?

11. Remember and describe one of your most memorable vacations with just the two of you. Get the photo albums out and look at them together.

12. Remember and describe one of your most memorable anniversaries.

Shared and Expressed Feelings

Sharing and expressing common feelings about things opens the final doorway to intimacy in friendships. This is a tricky area for some men, however, since they are generally not as emotional or expressive. Consider the following questions as they pertain to your marriage and answer accordingly.

13. Do you regularly spend time just talking with your husband? If so, when and where? Is there a special place you typically go?

14. What are the topics that come up most frequently? Do you take time to express or share your feelings, ideas, or plans? Is there equal talking time?

Closing Remarks

Some of these may seem pretty basic to you, but we can easily forget that husbands and wives should be friends too. Our husband is not just the father to our children or our spouse. When we don't foster our friendship with one another, the whole marriage suffers and can fall apart once the kids leave the nest. If you aren't having fun together, boredom and drudgery can set in. This can lead to feelings of restlessness, hopelessness, and even despair. Find time to remember your lives together – both the good times and the bad times. Schedule time to talk regularly and your relationship will blossom and flourish for years to come.

Daily Wrap-Up

In your own words, finish this sentence as it pertains to today's lesson: "If I am to follow *God's Radical Plan for Wives,* I need to work on…."

Think About This!

"Letting go of selfishness in order to support and build up the other person is how deep and lasting marriages are formed."

"Embracing his world will go a long way toward deepening your marriage."

Marriage Exercise #2

Remembering Your Journey Together

To remember your journey as a couple, select one of the activities below, or come up with your own. Commit to that activity.

1. Display pictures of good times together around your home.
2. Go through a box of old letters or mementos together.
3. Take turns recounting stories of shared experiences. Include your children.
4. Create a scrapbook together or a shadow box of significant mementos collected throughout your relationship.
5. Visit a place that is special or significant to you as a couple. First apartment? First date? Kiss? Place where you met?

Marriage Exercise #3

Talking Time

Talking and expressing yourselves with one another is a fundamental key to a healthy marriage. If you and your husband don't have a regular time each day or week to talk about feelings, ideas, or thoughts, then it is time to make that commitment. Date night, "couch-time," or an activity you enjoy doing together, like taking a walk after work, are perfect ways to talk as a couple. Try to make it something that works for your family and the stages of life they are in. Consider trading babysitting with another couple, if necessary, or talk after the kids go to bed.

Day 4—Becoming His Companion

1. Continue reading on pages 186-193 in *God's Radical Plan for Wives*.

2. Answer the following questions True (T) or False (F):

    _____ Men only need companionship from a few good buddies.

    _____ Wives intuitively know how to meet this companionship need in their husbands.

    _____ Becoming a companion that meets his need doesn't require much work from you.

    _____ The best way to meet this need in your husband is to find activities the two of you can enjoy together.

    _____ He may need a different kind of companionship from his wife for the various areas of his life.

Four Types of Companionship

3. There are four types of companionship that men desire from their wives. Next to each, write down a few traits, describing each one (see pages 179-182 in *God's Radical Plan for Wives*).

    a. Watcher/Listener:

    b. Cheerleader:

    c. Participant:

    d. Coach:

4. For each of the following descriptions, decide which of the four types of companionship is described. There can be overlap in your answers.
   (Watcher/Listener = W/L, Cheerleader = CL, Participant = P, Coach = C)

Descriptions	**Type**
Likes to strategize, think, and plan with you.	
Needs to be praised and built up.	
Participating in the event isn't needed; just spectating is fine.	
He needs to discuss it blow-by-blow while you actively listen.	
Has a need for active participation in the activity with him.	
Often asks, "What do you think?"	
Likes to be able to discuss the hobbies and activities you do together.	
Desires his good points to be pointed out to others.	
He needs you to lead and prod him to maximum success.	
Observation with focused attention on his activities is desired.	
A side-by-side participation is necessary.	
Your presence validates his importance.	
You are his source of strength and motivation.	
You are his biggest fan, strongest supporter.	

5. What kind of companionship do you think your husband needs from you? How do you know this?

6. Considering your answer and his need, are you meeting his need?

Closing Remarks

One secret to being a good companion to your husband is to identify and practice how he needs you to be his friend in the various parts of his life. Finding activities you both enjoy together, and supporting those he's involved with will significantly improve your marriage. Keep in mind *how* he needs you to be involved (watcher/listener, cheerleader, participant, or coach). The circumstances of your life may preclude you from being as involved as both of you would like but be creative and don't give up! Try to find what works best for both of you.

Daily Wrap-Up:

In your own words, finish this sentence as it pertains to today's lesson: "If I am to follow *God's Radical Plan for Wives,* I need to work on…."

> **Think About This!**
>
> "The godly wife understands her man's need for companionship and seeks to love him by meeting that need in the best way she can."
>
> "The companionship role may change from work, to recreation, or from home to social settings."

Marriage Exercise #4

Exploring Companionship Roles

Your husband desires for you to play a companionship role in the various areas of his life. Think of the four types of companionship we learned about and determine which applies to each situation ("X"). Then write down how you can practically apply it.

1. What type of companion does your husband generally desire you to be?

   Watcher/Listener _____   Participant _____
   Cheerleader _____   Coach _____

   Practical ways to apply this type of companionship:

2. What type of companion are you naturally?

   Watcher/Listener _____   Participant _____
   Cheerleader _____   Coach _____

3. Which companionship role does your husband want you to have toward his work?

   Watcher/Listener _____   Participant _____
   Cheerleader _____   Coach _____

   Practical ways to apply this type of companionship:

4. What companionship role does he need you to have toward his hobbies?

   Watcher/Listener _____   Participant _____
   Cheerleader _____   Coach _____

   Practical ways to apply this type of companionship:

5. Toward your finances?

   Watcher/Listener _____   Participant _____
   Cheerleader _____   Coach _____

   Practical ways to apply this type of companionship:

6. Toward church?

   Watcher/Listener _____   Participant _____
   Cheerleader   _____   Coach   _____

   Practical ways to apply this type of companionship:

7. Regarding community involvement?

   Watcher/Listener _____   Participant _____
   Cheerleader   _____   Coach   _____

   Practical ways to apply this type of companionship:

8. Toward his friends?

   Watcher/Listener _____   Participant _____
   Cheerleader   _____   Coach   _____

   Practical ways to apply this type of companionship:

9. Toward his internal/thought life?

   Watcher/Listener _____   Participant _____
   Cheerleader   _____   Coach   _____

   Practical ways to apply this type of companionship:

10. What is your husband's favorite recreational activity?

11. How does he want you to participate?

    Watcher/Listener _____   Participant _____
    Cheerleader   _____   Coach   _____

    Practical ways to apply this type of companionship:

Day 5—Friendship Warnings and Risks

Today we will look at warning signs and risks as they pertain to friendships with our husbands, other women, and people in our lives.

1. Finish reading pages 194-196 in *God's Radical Plan for Wives*.

2. To give some context to today's topics, look up the following verses in your Bible and record what they say to do or don't do.

   Ephesians 4:29

   Ephesians 5:3-4

   Ephesians 5:15-18

   1 Timothy 2:9-10

   1 Timothy 3:11 – *Note: Even though this verse speaks about the wives of deacons, the traits outlined describe those of a godly women and wives.*

Warning Signs and Risks Regarding Your Husband
According to the reading for today, answer the questions below.

3. When is it okay <u>not</u> to participate in an activity with your husband?

4. When you have determined that you cannot participate in an activity with your husband, what are the best steps to take? Put a "1" for the first step, a "2" for the second step, and a "3" for the third step.

155

_____ Suggest another activity or idea you would be willing to participate in with him instead.

_____ Determine the reason why you cannot participate in the activity—is it sinful or perverse? Does it cause you great anxiety or fear?

_____ Discuss your inability to participate in an activity with your husband in a loving and compassionate way.

5. Answer a "T" for True and an "F" for False to the following questions.

_____ A wife will more likely be listened to by her husband in these situations when she exposes his mistakes.

_____ Husbands more often than not respond to their wife's refusal to participate when she shows him compassion, care, love, and a desire to be with him.

_____ Refusal to participate in an activity doesn't necessarily mean limiting your husband's participation.

_____ If a husband wants his wife to participate in something that violates her conscience, she should yield to his desires.

_____ Participation in something that exposes your greatest fear should not be considered a part of being a godly wife.

Warning Signs and Risks Regarding Other Friendships
Women typically rely on other female friends to fill a need that her husband cannot meet. We have a need to talk, air out our feelings, disappointments, and struggles that men aren't necessarily equipped to understand. It is good for women to have a variety of different *female* friends. We benefit by having other women who keep us accountable in our marriages, our walk with God, and foster right thinking.

6. Write down the names of a few female friends who know you best.

7. What are some of the great qualities that these women have that you admire and what makes them a good friend?

Warning Signs and Risks with Ungodly Influences

As godly women, we need to exercise discretion when we choose our friends. There may be people in our lives that we know from work, neighborhoods, classes, the gym, or church that we may like and appreciate but may not want to confide in (see Proverbs 18:24). For example, as a married woman, other men should never be counted among your close friends. Also, be wary of women who draw you away from a godly life, or who discourage you from having godly relationships with your husband or kids. If you have "risky" people in your life that fit these descriptions, it would be best to limit (or even terminate) those relationships depending on how influential they are. As hard as that may be, it might be the best thing for your marriage (your first relationship after God).

8. Do you have people in your life that would be considered "risky"? Write down anyone you can think of that might fit this description. Then ask God how He would like you to proceed with that relationship.

9. Write down any traits or attributes that would cause them to be "risky" to you.

Warning Signs and Risks Regarding Ungodly Behaviors and Activities

Even if we do have many wonderful female friends that keep us in check, encourage us, pray for us, and lift us up to be the godly women and wives we are meant to be, there are still ways that our friendship activities can be harmful to our marriages. The examples below may be intuitive, but they can serve as a valuable reminder to help us keep guard over our marriages. That is not to say that these examples are absolutely harmful in and of themselves, provided proper boundaries are in place. Without good boundaries, however, they certainly can become threats to a good marriage.

Philippians 2:14-15 (NASB) reads, "Do all things without grumbling or disputing; so that you will prove yourselves to be blameless and innocent, children of God *above reproach* in the midst of a crooked and perverse generation, among whom you appear as lights in the world." The words *above reproach or beyond reproach* mean, "to be so good as to preclude any possibility of criticism."

10. How does this verse apply to the way a godly wife should conduct herself when she is with her friends and others?

157

11. How does Titus 2:3-5 communicate about how we should relate with our friends?

12. Write a "G" if this friendship activity can be *good* for your marriage or an "H" if this friendship activity can be potentially *harmful* to your marriage. *Note: Some can be both good and potentially harmful.*

   _____ Talking on the phone to your friends for several hours a day.

   _____ Accepting an invitation to go bar hopping or wine tasting with girlfriends.

   _____ Participation in groups where negative talk about husbands is typical.

   _____ Going away with girlfriends for a weekend that could get wild.

   _____ Accepting an invitation to lunch with a male co-worker.

   _____ Fostering friendships with other couples who are faithful in their marriages.

   _____ Participation in activities with girlfriends more often than with your husband.

   _____ Having friends on Facebook or other social media with men who are not your husband.

   _____ Putting your husband first before any other relationship.

A Prayer For Our Friendship...
Dear Heavenly Father, thank you that you built us for companionship. You designed us to be in relationship with other people, and you made it possible to have a built-in best friend in our marriage. Your Word says that You are our friend, and You won't ever leave us or forsake us. Help my husband and me to also be that kind of friend to each other. May we stick closer than a brother through good times and bad, loving each other in the best way possible.
In Jesus' Name,
Amen

Daily Wrap-Up

In your own words, finish this sentence as it pertains to today's lesson: "If I am to follow *God's Radical Plan for Wives,* I need to work on...."

Think About This!

Two secrets to a successful marriage: 1) Selfishness must go down; 2) Meeting the needs of your spouse must go up.

Weekly Wrap Up
In your own words, finish this sentence as it pertains to this week's lessons: "If I am to follow *God's Radical Plan for Wives,* I need to work on...."

Day 1:

Day 2:

Day 3:

Day 4:

Day 5:

What is the **#1 take-a-way** you had from this week's lesson?

Lesson 7

Chapter 8: Attractive Body & Soul

Lesson 7

Chapter 8—Attractive Soul & Body

Five Godly Beauty Secrets

B*eauty* can be a tough subject. For many women, it hits right to the core. This could be a very tough chapter to work through because many women don't think of themselves as beautiful. It can be hard to hear and receive it as truth. Have you ever reacted to someone who complimented your beauty with skepticism and suspicion? We struggle to believe it sometimes. But there is One who thinks we are very beautiful **all** of the time—with or without makeup, perfect clothes, or extra pounds. He loves us not just for our outer looks—or what we do or don't do for Him. We, beautiful woman, are God's *grand finale*—His "ta-da!" He is enamored with us in every way. He is crazy for us, and He loves us so much. We are truly lovely in His eyes.

All of us have very different ideas about what being "beautiful" is and what it isn't. The meaning of true beauty becomes warped over time. It's no wonder, when you consider the expectations our culture heaps on us every day through media, celebrities, and advertisements, along with how we generally feel about ourselves or how others have made us feel in the past. But because God created us and called us to Himself, **His** definition of beauty is what matters most.

Oftentimes our desire to *feel* beautiful can drive our actions, attitudes, and beliefs about ourselves. Many women strive harder to be more beautiful through extreme exercise regimens, diets, plastic surgery, fashion, beauty treatments, and so on – probably in response to the intense pressure to be outwardly "beautiful" by the *world's standard*. But I'm reminded in Romans 12:2, that as believers in Jesus Christ, we are not to be conformed to the pattern of this world. Rather, we are to be transformed by the renewing of our minds, which will be our aim this week.

This week I have outlined five beauty secrets for every godly woman to aspire to. Through God's Word we will begin to reprogram our minds to understand true beauty. Also, when we figure out what beauty is not, we can reset the expectations we hold for ourselves. Our goal as godly wives is to become wholly pleasing to God. When we do this, we become a woman our husband finds intoxicating—one he desires for years to come.

A Prayer for Beauty...

Lord, I praise you today for making me into the beautiful woman that you say I am. Your opinion matters above all others in the world. It's a gift that my husband loves me, and I want to continue pleasing him with both with my outer and inner beauty. Please continue to foster in me the inward attitudes of gentleness and a quiet spirit. Help me identify times when I repel rather than attract and to find a balance between the two in time, energy, and money. May I appreciate all that you've given me—my body, my situation, my strengths, and even my limitations. Ultimately, it's you who I desire to please.
In Jesus' Name,
Amen

Day 1—Beauty Secret #1: Cultivate a beautiful soul.

1. Begin this week's homework by reading pages 197-207 in *God's Radical Plan for Wives*.

2. After reading about *Rachel*, we see she is described as *captivating*. What traits made her "captivating" to her husband and others?

3. What is the key component of an attractive soul?

4. *Isabel* is another example of a *beautiful woman*. What are some of the words used to describe her?

Cultivating Inner Beauty

5. In your Bible, look up 1 Peter 3:3, 4.
   The Message version of verse 4 from the passage reads, "*Cultivate inner beauty, the gentle, gracious kind that God delights in.*" Look up the word *cultivate* in your dictionary and record the meaning below. Record several synonyms of the word.

   To cultivate:

   Synonyms:

   What do the definition and accompanying synonyms tell you about "inner beauty"?

   What does it require?

6. Answer the following questions True (T) or False (F):

   _____ Physical beauty is worthy of pursuing because it is long lasting. (See Proverbs 31:30)

   _____ The beauty of externals fades if the attitude of the heart is not beautiful.

   _____ As long as you are physically attractive, you will continue to attract your husband.

   _____ According to 1 Peter 3:3-4, women shouldn't wear jewelry, clothes, hairstyles, or elaborate adornment.

   _____ A woman should try to be attractive physically for her husband.

   _____ A beautiful soul is the secret to long-lasting beauty.

   _____ According to 1 Samuel 16:7, God says that He values our *inward* appearance more than external appearance.

7. Review the Marriage Exercise #1, pages 191-193 in *God's Radical Plan for Wives*. It describes nine aspects of a woman with "inner beauty." Spend some time looking them over and consider your answers.

Developing a Beautiful Soul

8. Describe what it means to create a "win" for your husband and why that would make you beautiful to him?

9. Looking at Marriage Exercise #2 in *God's Radical Plan for Wives*, what are three things a beautiful soul is or is not?

Possible Risks

10. What are some of the risks of not cultivating a beautiful soul?

Closing Remarks

Today, I want you to consider changes that may need to be made. This may be difficult and will require courage, faith, and effort on your part; but if you are serious about your marriage, you can do it! Take the answers you put down today seriously and activate your plans. The Bible says to "Commit your work to the Lord, and your plans will be established" (Proverbs 16:3). Take heart! God will help you with any honorable plans you have for your marriage.

Daily Wrap-Up

In your own words, finish this sentence as it pertains to today's lesson: "If I am to follow *God's Radical Plan for Wives,* I need to work on...."

Think About This!

"It is the beautiful soul that is the most attractive in the long term."

"Physical beauty is important, but this is not where you will continue to attract him."

"The beauty of externals fades if the attitude of the heart is not beautiful."

Day 2 —Beauty Secret #2: Attract, don't repel.

Have you ever been around a person who is a joy to be around? What about someone who is difficult? Today we will learn what it means to be someone who attracts others to us or repels them away. Prepare to dig deep as we examine core attributes of people who are either *attractive* or *repellant*. You can probably determine that it is critical to be a wife who attracts her husband in order to have a successful marriage.

1. Begin by reading page 1207-208 in *God's Radical Plan for Wives*.

Part I: The Core of One who "Attracts"

According to the Merriam-Webster dictionary, *attract* means "*To pull to or draw toward oneself or itself.*" In the reading for today, we learned that physical attractiveness may be something that initially attracted your man to you, but it is an attractive *soul* that keeps him close by.

2. In your dictionary, look up the following words and note their synonyms to further clarify the meaning of what "attracts" others to us.

   Grateful:

   Synonyms:

   Tranquil:

   Synonyms:

   Respectful:

   Synonyms:

   Flexible:

   Synonyms:

3. In your Bible, look up and record the following Scriptures that provide further emphasis on what an "attractive" wife looks like:

   1 Peter 3:1-6
   List several traits of an "attractive" wife.

   Proverbs 14:1

   Proverbs 16:24

   Proverbs 12:4(a)

   - What does the word *noble* mean? What is one with a "noble character" like?

   - In Bible times a crown was often a symbol of consecration, splendor, and dignity. How can a wife be *her husband's crown*?

4. **Extra: Proverbs 31** is worthy of studying all on its own. If you have time, read the passage and write about the characteristics this woman portrays as they relate to her husband on the lines below. It is important to note that she may represent the ideal woman, but her qualities are not meant to be 100% attainable (at least not without a full house staff).

   v. 10:

   v. 11:

   v. 12:

   v. 15:

   v. 21:

v. 24:

v. 25:

v. 26:

v. 27:

v. 28:

v. 30:

v. 31:

Part II: The Core of One who "Repels"
To understand something well, sometimes we have to look at the very opposite of what we are studying. According to Merriam-Webster, *repel* means *"to drive away, to discourage."*

5. In your dictionary, look up as many of the following words as you can, perhaps picking the ones that intrigue you the most or aren't as clear to you. Also, write down any synonyms that could further clarify the meaning of what "repels" people away from us.

   Contentiousness:

   Synonyms:

   Argumentative:

   Synonyms:

   Bitterness:

   Synonyms:

   Selfish:

   Synonyms:

Demanding:

Synonyms:

Prideful:

Synonyms:

Prickly:

Synonyms:

Defensive:

Synonyms:

6. We can even see examples of repellant wives in the Bible! Look up the following Scriptures that provide further emphasis on what a "repellant" wife looks like:

   Proverbs 12:4(b)

   Proverbs 21:9, 19

   Proverbs 27:15-16

Closing Remarks

I encourage you to spend some time completing the Marriage Exercise on the next page. Take a look at where your answers fall. The left side of the continuum is the "positive/attractive" side. If you found that many or most of your answers were toward this side, then you are doing great!

The right side is the "negative/repelling" side. If you found that many of your answers were more toward this side, it might be time to take a hard look at reasons for this. We don't set out to act in a repellant manner; in fact, we love our husbands and want to treat them well! But stress in life or hurts from our past can lead to bitterness and resentment, especially if we have not allowed time to process them thoroughly.

Not forgiving someone can have the same effect. If you have suffered from abuse (physical, emotional, verbal), past abortion(s), failed relationships, insecurities, a death, or a previous divorce, we highly recommend seeking professional counseling. At the very least, talk with a trusted Christian friend for help. The faster you engage the road to forgiveness, the faster healing begins.

Daily Wrap-Up

In your own words, finish this sentence as it pertains to today's lesson: "If I am to follow *God's Radical Plan for Wives,* I need to work on...."

Think About This!

"Giving into impulses of selfishness, laziness, pride, and envy can lead to the fading of outward beauty."

"A godly woman tries to forgive, digs for the positive, and allows God to deal with the rough edges of her husband."

Marriage Exercises #1

Do You Attract Or Repel?

Review the following questions. Consider how your husband might answer them. Put an "X" on the line where your answer falls. Try to be honest with yourself. An honest assessment is very helpful to reveal areas that may need work – both in your own life and in your husband's.

1. Does he enjoy being with you?

    AlwaysSometimesNot Really
    _____

2. Does spending time with you cause him to forget his problems or be reminded of them?

    Forget His ProblemsReminded of Them
    _____

3. When he is with you, does he feel that the world takes on a more positive glow or a more pessimistic slant?

    Positive GlowPessimistic Slant
    _____

4. Do you correct him when he does something wrong?

    Not ReallySometimesAlways
    _____

5. Do you complain about what he isn't doing or hasn't done yet?

    Not ReallySometimesAlways
    _____

6. Can he count on you to nag, criticize, or demand?

    Not ReallySometimesAlways
    _____

7. Do you value his opinion or ideas?

   Always   Sometimes   Not Really

   _____

8. Do you find new ways to spend money faster than it's coming in?

   Not Really   Sometimes   Always

   _____

9. Do you generally feel like the whole world treats you badly?

   Not Really   Sometimes   Always

   _____

10. Is bitterness evident in your life due to pain from hurts in your past?

    Not Really   Sometimes   Always

    _____

Scoring:

Take a look at where your answers fall. The left side of the continuum is the "positive and attractive" side. If you found that many or most of your answers were toward this side, then you are doing great!

The right side is the "negative and repelling" side. If you found that many of your answers were more toward this side, consider the reasons for this. Stress in life or hurts from the past lead to bitterness and resentment, especially if you have not allowed time to process them thoroughly. The effect is the same if you have not forgiven certain people in your life. If you have suffered from abuse (physical, emotional, verbal), past abortion(s), failed relationships, insecurities, a death, or a previous divorce, we highly recommend seeking professional counseling. At the very least, talk with a trusted Christian friend for help. The faster you engage the road to healing, the better.

Day 3—Beauty Secret #3: Adorn yourself with gentleness.

1. Read pages 209-212 in *God's Radical Plan for Wives*.

A Study of Gentleness
We learn in Scripture about two key qualities that God desires women to develop for beauty—*gentleness and a quiet spirit.* Today we will only focus on gentleness, camping on **1 Peter 3:1-6.** Let's see what God's Word says about why He wants women to be this way.

2. According to the text, the word *gentle* found in **1 Peter 3:4** is the Greek word *praus*. Put a checkmark in the box that best describes the meaning of this word:

    ☐ flexible   ☐ meek
    ☐ demanding   ☐ gentle
    ☐ weak   ☐ adaptable
    ☐ mild-mannered   ☐ hardened
    ☐ nagging   ☐ strong moral character

3. From the reading, answer the following questions True (T) or False (F).
    "A woman with a gentle spirit is like one who is…"

    _____ Willing to lower her expectations about what her husband will do, how the perfect vacation will look, or what perfect children are like

    _____ Flexible about all things, including her moral order

    _____ Willing to adjust quickly to non-essential areas in her husband's world in order to keep the relationship enjoyable and moving along

    _____ Not interested in adjusting her plans or expectations to incorporate new realities

    _____ Weak and limp

    _____ Gentle and non-demanding

    _____ Voluntarily flexible

    _____ One that becomes such a welcome part of her husband's life that he cannot imagine life without her

4. For the following questions, **1 Peter 3:1-6** is provided below in the *New American Standard Bible* (NASB) version to get the best word-for-word meaning from the text (try interchanging the word *submissive* with the word *adapt* to give greater meaning to the text):

1 In the same way, you wives, be submissive to your own husbands so that even if any of them are disobedient to the word, they may be won without a word by the behavior of their wives, 2 as they observe your chaste and respectful behavior. 3 Your adornment must not be merely external—braiding the hair, and wearing gold jewelry, or putting on dresses; 4 but let it be the hidden person of the heart, with the imperishable quality of a gentle and quiet spirit, which is precious in the sight of God. 5 For in this way in former times the holy women also, who hoped in God, used to adorn themselves, being submissive to their own husbands; 6 just as Sarah obeyed Abraham, calling him lord, and you have become her children if you do what is right without being frightened by any fear.

Who does verse 1 speak about winning over?

How do verses 1-2 specifically say they can be won over?

Why do you think this is the case?

Verse 3 addresses *adornment*. What does God say about external beauty?

Verse 4 talks about value of *the hidden person of the heart* with what two qualities?

How does verse 4 describe the quality of *gentleness and a quiet spirit*?

5. Is *gentleness and a quiet spirit* something we are born with like any other personality trait? Or is it a choice to be that way? Read verses 5-6. Look up the word *adorn* to further develop your answer. *Note who they put their hope in!*

Adorn:

6. In light of what we know to be important to God (John 3:16, 2 Peter 3:9), why are the characteristics of *gentleness and a quiet spirit* so precious to Him?

Closing Remarks

Was today's lesson profitable for you in understanding both the meaning and importance of gentleness? Gentleness is listed as one of the "Fruits of the Spirit," (Galatians 5:22-23) because it brings about a key result that God wants from our lives—drawing people to His saving grace. If *gentleness* is one of your key traits already, then take heart in knowing that this characteristic has Kingdom implications and you are contributing fruit! If you need work in this area, then take heart in knowing any time and effort spent developing this area is worthwhile and valuable.

Daily Wrap-Up

In your own words, finish this sentence as it pertains to today's lesson: "If I am to follow *God's Radical Plan for Wives,* I need to work on…."

Think About This!

"The Greek work for *gentle* does not have any weakness in it."

"Gentleness is a willingness to adapt and adjust one's expectations to God's will and to others' needs."

Marriage Exercises #2

Practicing Gentleness by Adapting Expectations

A large part of developing gentleness is how you handle expectations. A hope can become an expectation quickly. A rigid or excessively high expectation is what always leads to anger or some expression of selfishness. One insightful man said that anger is the result of unreasonable or unmet expectations. Unreasonable expectations and an unwillingness to adjust quickly are like huge warts on our soul. This inflexibility repels people. Life is a constant battle of expectations. It can be difficult to decide which ones are reasonable and which ones need to be adjusted.

1. How would your husband want you to be more flexible in order to fit more easily into his world?

2. In what areas are yours and his expectations at war?

3. How rigid are your expectations for your husband and family?

4. Do you find yourself getting angry often?

5. At what or whom do you get angry the most? What unmet expectation is behind this anger?

6. What are the expectations you have for your husband, family, and personal life?

7. Determine which ones need to be abandoned and which ones should be pursued with dogged persistence.

8. How clearly do you communicate those expectations?

9. Would your husband, family, and others agree with your expectations of them?

Day 4—Beauty Secret #4: Cultivate a quiet spirit.

1. Read pages 212-214 in *God's Radical Plan for Wives*.

A Study of the Quiet Spirit
The meaning of the term *quiet spirit* does not mean you have to remain quiet all the time. Your opinions, concerns, and frustrations are important; but there is a godly way to voice them. Let's look at today's lesson to see what a wife with a *quiet spirit* looks like and how this might impact her marriage.

2. In 1 Peter 3:4 are the words *quiet spirit*, which are the Greek words, *hesuchios pneuma*. Put a checkmark in the box that best describes the meaning of these words:

    ☐ calmness   ☐ harmonious
    ☐ emotional   ☐ encouraging
    ☐ argumentative   ☐ passionate/explosive
    ☐ peaceable   ☐ tranquil
    ☐ non-reactive   ☐ selfish

3. From the reading, answer the following questions True (T) or False (F).
   "A woman with a quiet spirit is like one who is…"

   _____ Able to bring calmness to any situation

   _____ A discourager and pessimistic

   _____ Emotional, defensive, and explosive

   _____ Like a sponge that dampens the fires of emotion in a situation

   _____ One who exacerbates the problem to prove a point or to get her way

   _____ Argumentative

   _____ One who can remain calm and harmonious in the midst of chaos

   _____ One who adds new clarity to a situation

   _____ Able to see problems in their proper perspective

   _____ One who stirs up conflict

4. From the reading, fill in the blanks below:

   a. "A quiet spirit means to add something that is _____

   _____ and _____ in its

   drawing power."

   b. When you are around a person with a biblical, quiet spirit, they add something new to you. What do they add?

5. Does someone with a quiet spirit attract or repel others?   ATTRACT   REPEL

6. Why or why not?

7. Can you think of someone you know who exemplifies a *quiet spirit*? How have they impacted your life?

8. Why might a woman with a "biblical, quiet spirit" be considered more attractive to her husband than one who is more fiery or emotional?

9. Read the following scenarios and answer as if they pertained to your husband. Think about the attributes in question 2 above and decide how a wife with a *gentle, quiet spirit* would respond to the following situations.

   He complains about something at home, work, or in his life.

   He wants you to do something that isn't your favorite thing to do or that doesn't seem fun or beneficial to you.

   He expresses anger over something bothering him, or he is having a bad day.

He asks you to do something you don't have time or energy to do.

He brings up something you did incorrectly or he corrects you.

He doesn't do something you've asked him to do, or he is unresponsive to a need you have.

10. How can you cultivate a *quiet spirit*? List several practical things you can do. Examples include prayer, exercise, avoiding over-commitment, setting boundaries, getting enough sleep, and so on.

Closing Remarks

In the Bible, there are several examples of people who exemplify a *quiet spirit*. One who stands out most to me is Mary, the mother of Jesus. What if Mary had a temperament that was overly emotional, demanding, or selfish? How might that have impacted Joseph's decision to marry her or affect the lengths he went to for her and her son? I imagine Mary to be a wife that was harmonious and reassuring to Joseph in the midst of their scorn, even during their dangerous escapes.

It is important to remember that having a *quiet spirit* does not mean you can never get angry or upset about something. Everyone does at times or we wouldn't be human. It comes down to the way we act toward the people in our lives and whether or not we value the condition of the relationship more than our own happiness, even if we feel wronged. We can choose to respond in a gentle and quiet manner, to not be easily offended, and not allow offenses to take us down. We can choose to communicate in a respectful, productive manner, and forgive. When we do, we portray an attractive and beautiful soul.

Daily Wrap-Up:

In your own words, finish this sentence as it pertains to today's lesson: "If I am to follow *God's Radical Plan for Wives,* I need to work on…."

> **Think About This**
>
> "A wife who can be the vessel of calm and harmony in the midst of chaos is a remarkably beautiful woman."
>
> "A woman with a beautiful and attractive soul does not exacerbate or add fuel to the fire but brings a calmness to any situation."

Marriage Exercises #3

Quiet Spirit, Positive Harmony, and Peace

1. Is a quiet spirit present in your marriage? To what degree? Consider if there is anyone stirring up conflict, increasing emotion or drama, or subtracting harmony.

2. Describe a time when you were selfish, angry, or demanding. Is this a typical response for you?

3. The quiet spirit is a positive trait that produces harmony, peace, encouragement, and the ability to see problems in their proper perspective. How have you done this in the last month?

4. What needs to be added to your husband's life that will bring him harmony and peace?

5. How can those things be added? Who are the people who can add those things?

Day 5—Beauty Secret #5: Examine motives for outer beauty.

Think about this sentence for a moment:

"When a wife focuses on her beauty, she should make sure the motive behind her actions is to strengthen her marriage."

We learned before that God values internal beauty more than outward beauty. However, He created men to be visually attracted to curves and the "femaleness" of women. Whether we can accept this or not, this visual attraction acts as a doorway through which deep and intimate love is achieved.

Some women tend to change their focus away from their outer beauty once married or shortly after the first child comes along. A woman who once took good care of her appearance suddenly shifts to one that is very functional or even sloppy. Admittedly, looking our best when we've been up all night with the baby or spit up on ten times a day is tough (and not very practical either). Some days we just don't feel beautiful or care much about our looks, so we don't put forth the effort to look nice. We figure that our husband will understand and will love us anyway. And surely they do during times of stress, like when a new child is born, or there is an illness in the home, and so on.

It can also go to the other extreme as well. A wife becomes obsessed with her looks to the point that it becomes her primary focus. Some women spend an incredible amount of the household's money on things like tanning, nails, hair care, cosmetics, health club memberships, implants, tattoos, and the latest fashions. I'm guilty of some of that; I'll admit it. The problem is in our motive. Who are we trying to impress? Why do we go to all the trouble and expense in money and time? What is it accomplishing?

I think when this happens it has a lot to do with our own insecurities, and our attempt to find self-worth in the culture's eyes. We may even try to convince ourselves it is all for our husband, but oftentimes our main motivation is to impress other women. We begin to compare ourselves to them and that can be dangerous. I'm not just talking about the Hollywood stars here. It can be the lady next to us in spin class or any other woman we run across. Our insecurity pricks at us, daring us to change to be more like her/them (outwardly). By dressing a certain way or participating in certain activities, we attempt to portray success, happiness, and having it all together. The more time our focus is on our outward appearance (which usually ends up catching the eyes of other men), the further away from godliness we can find ourselves.

Both of these approaches described above are detrimental to a successful marriage. Let's find out how a godly wife balances her outer and inward beauty to have the best marriage possible.

1. Finish reading pages 214-227 in *God's Radical Plan for Wives.*

2. From your reading, is there anything in particular that stands out? Is there anything you can relate to?

What does physical attractive mean?

3. What do we mean by being physically attractive?

4. What is beauty enhanced or confirmed by?

5. Who should a wife work to be attractive for?

Risks of Letting Yourself Go Physically

6. What are some of the risks of not maintaining physical attractiveness?

7. In your Bible, look up and record in your own words the key points of these verses as they pertain to our bodies.

    Romans 12:1-2

    1 Corinthians 6:19-20

    1 Timothy 2:9-10

8. Answer the following questions True (T) or False (F).

    _____ When women allow expectations of the culture to dominate their thoughts and actions, they can easily fall prey to obsessing over things that aren't pleasing to God (Romans 12:1-2).

_____ It is perfectly fine to cultivate your outer beauty as long as it isn't a major focus of your time and resources.

_____ Diminishing external attractiveness can often be a symptom of a negative, internal soul change.

_____ Remaining attractive, both inwardly and externally, is not necessary to maintain a successful, thriving marriage.

_____ Husbands feel loved when wives make an effort to attract or impress him.

_____ The key goal of marriage is for spouses to meet their own deepest needs rather than the deepest needs of the other person.

_____ The success of a woman depends on how other women think she looks.

_____ "My husband has no right to demand that I look presentable and attractive to him." (1 Corinthians 7:4)

_____ Wives can leverage their beauty and femininity to tame, direct, deepen, and develop their husbands.

_____ Wives have the right to not give into perverted or debasing sexual fantasies of their husbands.

Overemphasis on External Beauty
9. Is modesty important for married women? Why or why not? (1 Timothy 2:9, 10)

10. Do you consider yourself to be a woman who dresses modestly?   Yes   No

11. Consider your appearance and the level of care you take to maintain your external beauty. For each category, determine if it is an area of obsession for you or not – considering the amount of time and monetary resources you put toward it.

Are you obsessed?	**Yes or No**
Hair care: regular haircuts and styling, cleanliness and daily maintenance, budget conscious	
Use of make-up: modest use of make-up when appropriate, budget conscious	
Skin & nail care: Good hygiene, regular washing, facials as needed, hair removal, regular nail care, products, tanning, budget conscious	
Weight management: regular exercise, physical exertion, budget conscious	
Healthy eating: good eating habits, healthy and balanced meals, cooking at home, budget conscious, etc.	
Clothing and fashion: Stylish and clean looking, appropriate for circumstances, modesty, budget conscious	

12. Consider any changes you may need to make in any of these areas. You may want to ask your husband what he thinks. As women, we tend to be more critical of ourselves than we ought to be. Your husband may like everything just the way it is!

Changes to Make?	
Hair care	
Use of make-up	
Skin care	
Weight management	
Healthy eating	
Clothing and fashion	
Use of Color	
Modesty	

Closing Remarks

Good job this week! I know it required a lot of work and determination to get through all of the lessons. I'm so proud of you for persevering and pressing forward! I can't reiterate the importance of making sure you nurture both your inner beauty and outer beauty. It requires a balancing act to maintain both. Your inner beauty will develop to be more and more beautiful as you spend time in God's Word, in prayer, serving others, and surrendering things you struggle with to Him (Matthew 11:30). And your outer beauty will be just right for your husband when you take care of yourself within healthy boundaries and refuse to compare yourself to others. Keep striving to win his heart and you'll captivate him.

Daily Wrap-Up:

In your own words, finish this sentence as it pertains to today's lesson: "If I am to follow *God's Radical Plan for Wives,* I need to work on…."

> ### Think About This!
>
> "If a woman does not use her beauty and femininity to build a deep relationship with her husband, she has missed the point of the beauty God gave her."
>
> "Be attractive for the one you've committed to spend your life with."
>
> "A woman's beauty should be about the radiance of her virtue and not becoming a sexual object for her husband."

Weekly Wrap Up
In your own words, finish this sentence as it pertains to this week's lessons: "If I am to follow *God's Radical Plan for Wives,* I need to work on...."

Day 1:

Day 2:

Day 3:

Day 4:

Day 5:

What is the **#1 take-a-way** you had from this week's lesson?

Lesson 8

Chapter 9: Listening

Lesson 8

Chapter 9—Listening

Accessing His Soul

Did you know that the success or failure of a marriage, family relationships, or friendships sometimes comes down to our ability to listen? Listening well is one of the most important life lessons to learn for better relationships.

Listening to our husbands in a meaningful way requires two things that are very contrary to the nature of women: no interrupting or getting emotional. Learning to listen in an active-detached manner is probably the single most important lesson you will learn in this study. If you can learn to listen to your husband in this way, you will see immediate, positive results and an opening of his soul to you.

Day 1—Biblical Understanding of Listening

1. Begin this week's homework by reading pages 229-235 in *God's Radical Plan for Wives*.

2. After reading about *Susan,* what kind of listening signals did she give her husband whenever he talked? What was she hoping for?

3. Were there any parts of her story you could relate to regarding listening to your husband? Do you find listening to your husband easy or difficult?

4. From the reading, we see why someone with a "quiet spirit" is able to listening correctly. Summarize what you learned.

Biblical Understanding of the Need to Listen

5. Read and record **Proverbs 18:13.**

   ➤ According to this passage, how important is listening before answering? Why?

193

6. Read and record **James 1:19b-20**.

    ➢ According to this passage, how important is keeping your emotions stable and listening before speaking? Why?

7. In your dictionary, look up the following words and record the meaning that pertains to listening and hearing:

    Active

    Detached

8. Describe *active-detached* listening.

9. Answer the following questions True (T) or False (F):

    _____ Listening to your husband in a deep and meaningful way is a very natural process for wives.

    _____ When a man opens up, he is interested in a two-way conversation.

    _____ Being listened to in the right way is such a deep need of a man that he is willing to betray all that is dear just to be listened to.

    _____ Active, detached listening allows the husband to feel what they feel without demanding an explanation or response.

    _____ The wise woman listens and becomes the confessor for her husband.

    _____ The husband welcomes the wife who expresses her own feelings, thoughts, and opinions when he is trying to engage in deep, meaningful conversation.

    _____ As his confidant, he needs to be able to express his insecurities, fears, dreams, and scars without judgment.

Closing Remarks

Hopefully this lesson helped you to better understand what it means to listen actively in a detached, non-reactive manner, and why this type of listening is so important to your husband's life. As we continue with our lesson, you will learn how to be a great listener and can practice the application exercises. Listening is definitely a skill to be honed but once mastered, it can be applied to all of your relationships. The work you put into this skill will pay dividends in your marriage and life.

Daily Wrap-Up:

In your own words, finish this sentence as it pertains to today's lesson: "If I am to follow *God's Radical Plan for Wives,* I need to work on...."

Think About This!

"Most women long for an intimate marriage, but they need to realize that the way they listen can make or break this longing."

"A wise woman's security cannot come from her husband alone. She must place her trust, focus, and security entirely on God."

"When a wife allows her man to vent his feelings without an emotional reaction from her, it connects them in ways never imagined."

Day 2—Become a Great Listener

Believe it or not, a wife who listens well can exert more influence in her husband's life than one who does most of the talking. When we listen, we gain access to the inner workings of his heart and mind. Want to change your husband? Then become a wife who listens deeply without reacting. We call it active, detached (or non-reactive) listening; and it is a life-long skill that everyone would do well to master.

1. Begin this week's homework by reading pages 235-242 in *God's Radical Plan for Wives.*

Becoming a Great Listener

2. What is the key idea in good listening?

3. What is the goal of listening to your husband?

4. Why is listening to your husband sometimes a challenge?

Risks of Not Listening Well

5. What is the risk of not listening deeply to your husband in an active-detached manner?

6. What can you do to demonstrate that you are engaging in the topic of conversation in a meaningful way? List five characteristics of good listening:

    -
    -
    -
    -
    -

6. Answer the following questions True (T) or False (F):

   _____ As a wife listens to her husband, her feelings about the topic of conversation are important to vocalize right at that time.

   _____ Active, detached listening is a life-long learning assignment.

   _____ Good listeners pay more attention to what the person means to say, not the accuracy of what is being said.

   _____ A *godly wife* accepts the challenge of developing her soul to the point where nothing anyone can say will cause her to react.

   _____ Men are not capable of talking deeply about their feelings, fears, and emotions.

   _____ Active, detached listening is a lot like talking to teenagers. They want you to listen; but they don't want you to react, power up, or shut down what they are thinking.

The Problem of Betrayal

From the reading, we learned that the word *gossip* is the word *diabolos*, which means *slanderer* or *devil-like one*. If you want to maintain intimacy with your husband, you must know how to keep a confidence. This goes for any relationship for that matter. A trustworthy partner is crucial to an intimate relationship. Most husbands would never share a personal matter with their wives if they knew that they turned around and told other people about them.

7. In your Bible, look up the following verses and record what it says specifically about wives on the lines below:

   1 Timothy 3:11

   * When the Apostle Paul wrote this verse, he was referring to the wives of deacons. He expects them to be as trustworthy and respectable as a deacon would need to be to serve in this way. A godly wife must not engage in gossiping about the activities her husband is involved in.

   Proverbs 11:13

8. Describe the harm that can happen when a wife discusses the affairs of her husband and the marriage.

9. Is it ever acceptable to talk to someone about what he says or does to you?

10. Whom have you shared intimate details about your husband with? Is there anyone you are tempted to share with?

11. Are there women you know who are prone to talking about their husbands? If so, you may need to consider how your interactions with them may need to change. Don't be fooled into thinking that it is acceptable to disrespect your husband by talking negatively about him.

12. Are there women you know who never say anything bad about their husbands? Would you consider them a good influence or role model for you? If so, how can you draw closer to them?

13. Do you discuss your husband's faults? If so, confess your sin to the LORD and repent. Begin talking about your husband's good points and determine to be one of his biggest fans! Remind yourself of his strengths from the first week of the study.

Why was it easier to listen before marriage?
14. What happens in a relationship that makes listening to each other harder over time?

15. Was listening to your husband easier before marriage? If so, why?

Daily Wrap-Up:

In your own words, finish this sentence as it pertains to today's lesson: "If I am to follow *God's Radical Plan for Wives,* I need to work on…."

Think About This!

"If your husband hears that what he shares with you is repeated, he stops sharing because you're not a safe person to him."

"Most bad ideas will be exposed if you probe for enough facts."

"It is the wise woman who realizes that what she won him with is what he still expects today."

Marriage Exercise #1

Active, Non-Reactive Techniques

By practicing a few non-reactive techniques, you can be ready for times when you are listening to your husband and feel the urge to react. Start by reading Marriage Exercise #1 in *God's Radical Plan for Wives*. Write down a few ways to respond to the following scenarios with active detachment. I wrote down a sample negative and positive response for you so you can see what we are looking for.

1. *"Honey, I just really can't take my job anymore. My boss is horrible, I'm working too hard, and the pay isn't great. I'm thinking of starting my own business..."*

    a. Sample negative response:
    What? That's crazy! You can't start your own business; we've got mouths to feed! Just suck it up and get over it already. You're overreacting.

    Sample positive response:
    Wow! Starting your own business. That's a big deal. It sounds like you are fed up with your boss! What's going on?

    b. Your positive response:

2. *"Honey, I don't want us hanging out with Mark and Monica anymore. I know she's your best friend, but the guy's a jerk and I have nothing in common with him."*

    Your positive response:

3. *"Sweetheart, Bob asked me to go to Spain with him for a month with the guys and I think I want to go. I've been needing some time to myself and this is the perfect thing."*

    Your positive response:

4. *"Babe, I love you, but I just don't think I want to be married anymore."*

   Your positive response:

5. *"I can't wait to show you the new boat I bought. You're never going to believe the great deal I got on it!"*

   Your positive response:

6. Think of a scenario of your own.

   Your positive response:

Day 3—Developing Listening Skills: Part I

Today is the day where we learn how to apply important skills that will add tremendous value to any relationship. If you want people – especially your husband – to know that they are truly valuable to you, putting these skills into practice will do the trick. These techniques could be practiced over your lifetime. You won't be perfect every time, but eventually it will dawn on you that you're not listening very well and you can go back and try again. You will be given exercises to practice each skill, so finding a good friend or classmate to work with will help. Have fun with it!

1. Read pages 242-249 in *God's Radical Plan for Wives*.

Honing Your Listening Skills

2. What do good listening techniques communicate?

3. List the four listening skills listed in today's reading.

    -
    -
    -
    -

Maintaining eye contact

4. Think about a time when you have been talking to someone, and they won't make eye contact with you. What does it say to you about them? How does it make you feel?

5. What does making "eye contact" communicate to a person who is talking?

#1: Practice making and holding eye contact
Next time your husband or one of the kids comes into a room and starts talking to you, stop what you're doing and make eye contact with them. While they are talking, resist the urge to continue with what you are doing until they are finished. *(Note: I don't mean for you to stare them down in a creepy way; just show them that you are paying attention by looking at them.)*

Positive body language

6. How important is body language in a conversation?

7. What body position best signals how much you want to listen?

8. Consider these positive and negative body positions. Write down what they communicate to someone who is talking to you.

   Folding your arms:

   Looking at them:

   Slouching, either sitting or standing:

   Leaning forward while sitting:

   Wringing your hands or twiddling your thumbs:

   Fidgeting with something:

   Looking around:

   Nodding your head slightly:

   Interrupting or allowing someone else to interrupt:

   Playing with or looking at your cell phone:

#2: Practice positive body language
When you and your husband begin to engage in a conversation, try practicing positive body language tendencies, such as leaning toward him slightly when he is talking. Other ideas would be to look at him fully, nodding your head slightly, etc.

Use minimal encouragers

9. What are "minimal encouragers" and what do they communicate?

10. Can you think of a time when you were talking to someone and they were absolutely silent? Describe the feeling you got while you were talking:

11. Write down 3-5 "minimal encouragers" that you often use or will begin to use, to communicate interest in the conversation.

#3: Practice using minimal encouragers
Next time you have a conversation with your husband, interject the use of minimal encouragers. Try to show more facial reaction and begin to watch what happens.

Engage the conversation with verbal following
12. What is the key idea behind "Verbal Following?"

13. What is the potential risk of not following the subject or topic while someone is talking? Have you ever been made to feel that way by someone?

#4: Practice verbal following
During your next conversation with your husband, practice "verbal following" by disciplining yourself to not change the subject to another topic or idea that pops into your mind. In addition, practice not interjecting your own thoughts or opinions into the discussion. Try to focus solely on his topic of choice.

Closing Remarks

Today you have learned about four very valuable listening skills: making and holding eye contact, the importance of positive body language, using minimal encouragers, and verbal following. Pick one of these skills and put it into practice. If you are able, purpose a conversation with your husband tonight and put all four into practice. You'll be amazed at how a few simple skills can make a difference. Tomorrow we will cover three additional skills and then put them all to the test with some practice scenarios.

Daily Wrap-Up:

In your own words, finish this sentence as it pertains to today's lesson: "If I am to follow *God's Radical Plan for Wives,* I need to work on…."

> **Think About This!**
>
> "There are only a few things that cause a husband to want to please his wife—one is having a soul mate who will listen to the whole of his world."
>
> "If you are skilled at listening, you can guide your husband into opening up areas of his life."

Day 4—Developing Listening Skills: Part II

Counselors help draw out the heart of the person by using the skills we will cover today. Don't be intimidated if they seem counterintuitive or hard to implement at first. With practice you will get better with each conversation. To practice, find a good friend or classmate to work with.

1. Read pages 249-253 in *God's Radical Plan for Wives*.

Asking follow-up questions

2. What does asking follow-up questions accomplish in a conversation?

3. When might you use this technique in a conversation?

4. How difficult is it for you to not insert your own thoughts, ideas, or opinions into a conversation – especially when you know something about the subject? What can you do to stop yourself from interjecting or interrupting?

#1: Practice asking follow-up questions
When you and your husband begin a conversation, try to clarify or find out more about his topic by only asking questions. Refrain from stating your opinions even if you think you already know the answer. Watch for times when you formulate responses in your mind; instead, refocus on what things you would like to know and formulate questions to ask.

Paraphrasing (also called reflecting back)

5. What is the idea behind "paraphrasing?"

6. What is the key to good "paraphrasing?"

7. When might you use this technique in a conversation?

#2: Practice paraphrasing/reflecting back

Next time the person you are talking to is emotional, try paraphrasing or reflecting back the things they are saying in order to draw more from them. This is especially useful when talking to teenagers or someone trying to process a problem or idea they have. Using the example sentence, "I hate my life. I just want to quit everything," paraphrasing or reflecting back might look like, "Wow, you sound really frustrated. What happened today? Want to talk about it?"

Summarizing
8. What is the idea behind "summarizing?"

9. When and how is "summarizing" best used?

#3: Practice summarizing
Next time your husband is trying to process a problem or idea, try summarizing what he says back to him. Periodically ask, "Let me see if I understand what you're saying…" followed by a summary of 2-3 thoughts about what you think he means.

Daily Wrap-Up:
In your own words, finish this sentence as it pertains to today's lesson: "If I am to follow *God's Radical Plan for Wives,* I need to work on…."

Think About This!

"The most important thing you can say to your mate is 'I love you,' and you say that by listening well."

"When your husband is allowed to emote in a safe environment and sort through his emotions out loud, he can respond more effectively to his problems."

"By listening well, you are ministering to your husband, not gaining information for yourself."

Marriage Exercise #2

Putting It All Together

Let's work to connect all that you've learned in this chapter. Read the following scenarios. Using the seven listening techniques, rehearse in your mind what you would do to communicate the value you place on the person speaking to you. The goal is for them to come away believing they are valuable and that you were interested in what they had to say. Think about communicating your care for them even if circumstances may not be optimal. Write down your strategy on the lines below.

1. You are having a face-to-face conversation with a friend who begins to talk about a subject you are not really interested in.

2. Your husband is in a talkative mood, but you have things to accomplish before bed.

3. A person you know sees you at the grocery store and starts a conversation. It's busy all around you, but the person seems very intent on talking.

4. You are having a face-to-face conversation with a friend who is trying to process a problem or idea they have.

5. Your teenager or husband starts to talk about things that alarm you. It's hard to react without shock or surprise.

Day 5 — Listening in Your Marriage

It takes time to develop good listening skills, but they are a worthwhile investment of your time and energy. Once you've mastered a few of them, I'm confident you will see a remarkable difference in the quality and depth of your relationships. Since our focus is on bettering the relationship with your husband, let's take a look at ways to make listening work in your marriage.

1. Read pages 253-256 in *God's Radical Plan for Wives*.

Maintaining Emotional Distance

2. Describe what it means to maintain emotional distance when listening to your husband. Why is this important to do especially as it pertains to your husband?

Focus your Attention on Listening

3. Listening without reacting requires your full attention. What are things you could do, when your husband is talking, to demonstrate he has your full attention?

Discuss Reactions Later

4. It's normal to have strong feelings to things that are being said. How would strong reactions be best handled?

5. Explain the two-hour/two-day rule. Is this something that could benefit you and your husband?

Undistracted Listening Times

6. Every marriage needs to find regular, undistracted times to talk. What are some good examples of undistracted listening times for your marriage? What do you currently do? How does it work? What could you do to make it even better?

Minimize Distractions

7. What can you do to minimize distractions in your home so that you can have productive talking time with your husband?

Sobering Issues

8. How are a man's and a woman's idea of talking different?

9. What does a man require if he is going to open up? What can you do to get him to open up?

10. What does it mean to have a "sober mind" when listening to your husband?

Hearing Disturbing Things

11. When is it okay not to listen to your husband? How can this be handled while maintaining his dignity?

A Prayer for Connection…

Lord, help me to be a good listener and partner to my husband. Slow down my thoughts and my impulses to interrupt, voice my opinion or concerns, or change topics. Allow my ability to listen draw him out so that he can express his feelings and ideas without criticism or rejection. Let me be the "safe" one he can rely on to talk things out. God, could you help us to find regular time to talk as a couple? It's so important that we connect every day, every week, every month, and every year. We desire to be a couple in touch with each other, but we will need your help with the children, the finances, and our schedules. We commit them to you. In Jesus's Name, Amen

Daily Wrap-Up:

In your own words, finish this sentence as it pertains to today's lesson: "If I am to follow *God's Radical Plan for Wives,* I need to work on…."

> ### Think About This!
>
> "A man will be irresistibly drawn to a woman who allows him to tell his story, no matter how convoluted, contrived, and masculine it is."
>
> "There are very few things a woman can do that is as rewarding to her husband as listening with focused, detached attention."

Marriage Exercise #3

Purposing Time To Listen

Every marriage needs regular time to have uninterrupted conversations. This can be very difficult when small children are in the house. Here are a few practical ideas for various situations. Read the ideas below and think about which of these could apply to you. In the lines below, write out a plan and propose it to your husband. Start one of them right away, adding one or two as you find opportunity.

1. **Devotional Time and Prayer**
   Wake up early together to spend 15-30 minutes to pray, read scripture, and share quiet time together. Try challenging each other to memorize scripture passages or serve the Lord together.

2. **Couch Time**
   As soon as your husband walks in the door, set aside 15-30 minutes to talk before dinner. This time would primarily be used for downloading the events of the day and communicating about any plans for the evening. Doing this regularly conditions the kids to accept it. They will generally begin to leave you alone during this time spent together.

3. **Taking Walks**
   Walking either first thing in the morning or evening is a great way to engage in deeper conversation. A walk takes both parties away from distractions around the house. Children can come in strollers or on bikes, though sensitive topics would need to be limited.

4. **Right After Dinner**
   Family conversation after the evening meal is a great time to talk. To be effective, don't rush into the next activity or begin chores right away. Make it early enough so the kids don't have to rush out after the last bite is consumed. For adult time, dismiss the children and do the dishes together.

5. **Pillow Time**
   Spending 10-15 minutes before turning out the lights can be a great way to summarize the day or look ahead to tomorrow. Avoid stressful topics, like finances, as it can cause sleeplessness or anxiety.

6. **Weekly, Monthly, Quarterly, and Annual Time Together**
   It is extremely important for parents to find a way to spend one-on-one time together as a couple.

Weekly Wrap Up
In your own words, finish this sentence as it pertains to this week's lessons: "If I am to follow *God's Radical Plan for Wives,* I need to work on...."

Day 1:

Day 2:

Day 3:

Day 4:

Day 5:

What is the **#1 take-a-way** you had from this week's lesson?

Lesson 9

Conclusion

Lesson 9

Conclusion

As we wrap up our study on *God's Radical Plan for Wives,* we have found that this book is in essence a job description for married women. All of the topics should be worked on over the course of your marriage to gain credibility with your husband and promote a willingness to change. It takes a *godly wife* to recognize that she may be part of the problem and identify what can be done differently. By doing what God's Word says, you can safeguard you marriage or even salvage it.

For a wife, her work in the marriage is to continue meeting the needs of her husband even after the fun and joy of dating is over. If you want your marriage to work at a new level, you must meet his needs. If you want to gain leverage (effectiveness or influence) to help your husband reach his full potential, then simply strive to meet his needs. Plus, by doing so, you might eliminate a few annoying habits along the way! Meeting his needs is the work of a marriage relationship from the woman's side. By meeting his needs, he will begin to meet yours. It is a means to an end.

Often times, it is the simple act of one person fulfilling a God-given role to get a marriage moving forward again. Why not let it begin with you? Wives who embrace their marriage as a huge part of their life acknowledge that they have a responsibility in that relationship to make it succeed. By focusing on the requirements of a wife's role and ministering to a husband's needs, she can foster a marriage of great joy. Let's finish out this last week of study and see what last bits we can glean. There will only be three days assigned, but Day 3 could be extended to take more time if needed.

There are several summarizing exercises toward the end of the book that I encourage you to complete as well. Any work you can do summarizing the lessons learned over the past eight weeks will help solidify and cement your thoughts and ideas about how you've changed, areas to refocus on, and so on. Hang in there with this last week of study; I promise it will be worth your while.

Day 1—Biblical Understanding of Listening

1. Read pages 257-260 in *God's Radical Plan for Wives.*

2. From your reading, discuss Beth's strategy on getting her husband back. Think about what you would do or wouldn't do differently.

3. Consider Regina and her marriage. Do you know a couple like this or a wife that fits this description? What can you learn from her?

4. What is your response to the following quote from the reading regarding Beth and Regina? *"It is their full embrace of the role and duties of a wife that allows them to enjoy a marriage of great joy."* Does this describe you in any way?

Daily Wrap-Up:

In your own words, finish this sentence as it pertains to today's lesson: "If I am to follow *God's Radical Plan for Wives,* I need to work on…."

Think About This!

"As she lives out her role of being a wife, every woman will express it differently and with wonderful uniqueness."

"She chose to fight for the future of her family and for her husband. She is a godly wife."

Day 2—The Awful Wife

It is important to understand if a wife is meeting her husband's needs or not. One way to do this is by looking at examples of what we would describe as an *awful wife*. You may wonder how this wife's husband could be attracted to her. You might know women like this, or you may even see some of these characteristics in yourself. Remember, even if you do, it is not too late to make some changes. Commit to a new beginning today.

1. Finish reading pages 260-261 in *God's Radical Plan for Wives*.

2. Evaluate the scenarios below. Determine if you currently do this or have done this in the past. What changes did you make or will begin to implement today? **Think about what a godly wife would do instead and add that on the lines below.**

   Scenario #1
   An awful wife may belittle her husband to others or even to his face in multiple ways by replaying his failures, weaknesses, and shortcomings. What would a godly wife do instead?

   Scenario #2
   An awful wife may be demanding, inflexible, or refuse to consider she could be wrong. In most cases, her opinions and decisions must win. What would a godly wife do instead?

   Scenario #3
   An awful wife may be helpless, lazy, and overspending. She may be self-focused on her career, hobbies, friends, or appearance, possibly leaving the home, family, and marriage in disarray. What would a godly wife do instead?

Scenario #4
An awful wife may refuse to honor her husband's interest in physical intimacy, making sex a reward for good behavior or with so little frequency that he rarely expects to be intimate with her. What would a godly wife do instead?

Scenario #5
An awful wife may create a world full of selfish or feminine pursuits, refusing to converse or participate in any areas he enjoys. She may even belittle his likes and interests. What would a godly wife do instead?

Scenario #6
An awful wife may be quick to complain. She is ungrateful, inflexible, critical, demanding, self-centered, bossy, and either neglectful or overindulgent of her appearance. What would a godly wife do instead?

Scenario #7
An awful wife does not listen to her husband. She finishes his sentences; changes the subject to something more interesting to her; is quick to react openly to what he is saying; and displays boredom with his topics, feelings, ideas, and concerns. What would a godly wife do instead?

Daily Wrap-Up:

In your own words, finish this sentence as it pertains to today's lesson: "If I am to follow *God's Radical Plan for Wives,* I need to work on...."

> **Think About This!**
>
> If any of these describe you in any way, it is not an accurate excuse to say that he makes you like this. You are choosing to respond to what is around you with these responses. The good news is that you don't have to continue being like that. With God's help, He can help you see where and how to change.

Day 3—Reflection

This day's homework is designed for reflection so that you can see the progress you've made from week one to this last week. It should remind you of how far you've come and help you prioritize the work still to be done.

1. Beginning with Week 1, write down the summary answer you developed for the question: *"What is the #1 take-a-way you had from this week's lesson?"* If you didn't fill it in, then spend some time going back through the lessons and do a quick recap.

   Week #1—Introduction, Chapter 1, Chapter 2

   Week #2—Respect

   Week #3—Adapting

   Week #4—Domestic Leadership

Week #5—Intimacy

Week #6—Companionship

Week #7— Attractive Soul and Body

Week #8— Listening

2. Prioritize the topics for your marriage numbering them 1-7 with "1" for the most important topic to address and a "7" for the least important topic to address.

   _____ Respect

   _____ Adapt

   _____ Domestic Leadership

   _____ Intimacy

   _____ Companionship

   _____ Attractive Body and Soul

   _____ Listening

3. What are some action items you can take for your top three priorities?

   Priority #1:

   Priority #2:

   Priority #3:

Closing Remarks

You've been given a lot to think about. Wonderful isn't it? Knowing that there is a huge amount of information in this book, I would encourage you to take your time on some of these exercises. Remember to prayerfully ask God to direct you to the godly wife quality He would like you to work on at the time. Focus on just one until it feels natural or comfortable and remember to implement the things you have already practiced. Take things one at a time and let this be a journey. Trust God! He made you to be your husband's friend, lover, and closest confidante. Only <u>you</u> can do it! May God bless you abundantly on your journey.

Appendix

1. Five Problems of Marriage Chart
2. Five Problems of Marriage
3. The Godly Wife—Meeting His Needs
4. The Godly Husband—How to Really Love Her

The Five Problems of Marriage Chart
Source: *Marital Intelligence* by Dr. Gil Stieglitz

Ignoring Needs	Immature Behaviors	Clashing Temperaments	Competing Relationships	Past Baggage
Wife's Needs	**Level 1**	Male vs. Female	God	**Type 1**
Honor	Thoughtless			Victimization
Understanding	Immaturity	Myers-Briggs	Self	
Security	**Level 2**	Temperament		**Type 2**
Building Unity	Directed		Marriage	Family and
Agreement	Immaturity	Ancient		Cultural
Nurture	**Level 3**	Temperaments	Family	Programming
Defender	Destructive or			
	Addictive	Love Languages	Work	**Type 3**
Husband's Needs	Immaturity			Past Actions
Respect			Church	
Adapt	**Eight Solutions**			
Domestic	Stop further		Money	
Leadership	immaturity			
Intimacy	Apology		Society	
Companionship	Alignment			
Attractive Soul	Thoughtful requests		Friends	
and Body	More love			
Listener	Change Behavior		Enemies	
	Clarify			
	Patience			

2

The Five Problems of Marriage

(Taken from *Marital Intelligence*, by Gil Stieglitz)

To be intelligent about marriage, we must identify the key problems and implement practical solutions that will inject new levels of happiness, love, and joy into the marriage through positive actions.

1. **Ignoring needs**
   For Husbands—*God's Radical Plan for Wives* (See Appendix 3)
   R: Respect
   A: Adapt
   D: Domestic Leadership
   I: Intimacy
   C: Companionship
   A: Attractive Soul and Body
   L: Listening

   For Wives—*God's Radical Plan for Husbands* (See Appendix 4)
   H: Honor
   U: Understanding
   S: Security
   B: Building Unity
   A: Agreement
   N: Nurture
   D: Defender

2. **Immature behaviors (three levels):**
   Level 1: Those behaviors that are a part of everyday life; they usually come as a shock after the wedding.
   Not picking up his clothes
   She constantly interrupts
   His control over the TV remote
   She is always late
   He is moody and insensitive
   She is negative or gossips

   Level 2: Those actions that are specifically aimed at your marriage partner either for punishment or to gain control.
   Sarcasm, ridicule, slander
   Silence
   Spending
   Acting sick or sleeping a lot to avoid confrontation

Acting/retaliating disproportionately to the situation
Selfishness, considering one's own needs
Accusations/blaming
Anger, controlling

Level 3: Highly destructive and can permanently damage a relationship or life.
Adultery
Drug Use
Abuse
Criminal behavior
Drunkenness
Violence

3. **Clashing temperaments**
   Temperament is the consistent tendencies, patterns, reactions, and internal impulses that are part of one's normal actions and responses to life. They factor in to who we are and what we are like. Often, qualities that attracted us to our spouse can often begin to repel! We can only have great marriages if we accept our differences and try to adapt to them.

4. **Competing relationships**
   This is a matter of understanding the order of our relationships and prioritizing our time accordingly. A marriage requires a commitment of time, energy, and resources just to survive – let alone to grow. Learning to place a high priority on the marriage reaps huge results in the health of the marriage.

5. **Past baggage**
   These are wounds and destructive internalized programming, as well as guilt and consequences from our past actions. They include wounds, hurts, abuse, victimization, negative family or cultural programming, and past actions. Unless wounds are exposed, grieved, and processed, the marriage suffers.

3

The Godly Wife
Meeting His Needs

R	Respect	A godly wife, more than any other person in his life, provides the respect and admiration her husband needs.
A	Adapt	A godly wife adapts her strengths to make up for the weak areas of her husband. Her goal is to adapt to who he is and finding a way to work together for a healthy and productive marriage.
D	Domestic Leadership	A godly wife understands the importance of a focused attention on home for the lives of her husband and family. She uses her unique skills and abilities to manage domestic affairs of the home.
I	Intimacy	A godly wife chooses to love her husband intimately, embracing his needs as the definition of what it means to love him.
C	Companionship	A godly wife recognizes that the key to a man's soul is by joining him in his hobby, work, or passion.
A	Attractive Soul and Body	A godly wife focuses on a balance between physical beauty and a beautiful soul. Her time is spent developing a gentle and quiet spirit – the greatest beauty secret. Physically, she is beautiful for her husband, not competing with other women or for the attentions of other men.
L	Listening	A godly wife listens to her husband with an active detachment, allowing him to feel what he feels without demanding a response.

4
The Godly Husband
How to Really Love His Wife

H	Honor	A godly husband chooses his wife as his number one priority, respecting and valuing the woman she was created to be.
U	Understanding	A godly husband seeks to live with his wife in an understanding way.
S	Security	A godly husband responds to his wife's need for security and stability so she can maintain her connection to him in the marriage.
B	Building Unity	A godly husband accepts responsibility for developing unity in the marriage and family and cherishes his wife with all of her strengths and weaknesses.
A	Agreement	A godly husband strives to become one-minded with his wife by involving her in decision-making. He seeks the wisdom that God communicates through her.
N	Nurture	A godly husband looks after his wife's spiritual, mental, emotional, and physical needs, allowing her to reach her full potential.
D	Defender	A godly husband accepts the responsibility to lovingly defend his wife against others, herself, her desires, and her fears.

Leader's Guide

The study can be done as a personal study, in a small-group format, or with a partner or mentor. Each student will need a copy of *God's Radical Plan for Wives*, by Gil & Dana Stieglitz, as well as a copy of *God's Radical Plan for Wives Companion Bible Study*, by Jennifer Edwards. Materials can be ordered at www.ptlb.com.

Personal Study

This material works great for an individual, deep, personal study of *God's Radical Plan for Wives.* We recommend that you take each chapter slowly in your own time. First, do the reading in the book, followed by the daily study questions. Complete each of the exercises before moving on to the next chapter. Attempt to do as many of the Marriage Exercises as possible and put what you learn into practice. *Recognize that you won't be able to change everything all at once.* It takes time and practice. Go back and re-read pages as needed, adding to your journal any thoughts you have, progress you've made, things to come back to, and so on. Use this experience as a time of self-growth that will greatly benefit you and everyone in your family.

After you complete the study, you may want to consider asking another woman who you think exemplifies the "godly wife" to be an accountability partner with you. Or perhaps she could go through the study with you. Consider who in your life might benefit from the insights gleaned in this book, sharing what you learn with other wives or friends. Who knows? Maybe you will lead a small group study of your own!

Remember God loves you and your marriage is one of His highest priorities. Be encouraged that the time and energy you spend working through this book will never be wasted. Submit your plans to the Lord and get ready to see a mighty work in your marriage.

Group Study

Ten weeks should be allotted for a group study—an introductory session and nine additional sessions that correspond to the chapters in *God's Radical Plan for Wives*. To do this study as a group, consider the ideal size that would best achieve the maximum benefit of sharing and accountability. If the class is larger, consider breaking into smaller groups of 7-8 women to promote discussion and accountability.

A good class format for this material lasts an hour and a half and divides the class into three segments. After starting with prayer, the first segment should be spent reviewing the key points and message from the week before, followed by a review of the homework (50 minutes). Discuss the Scripture passages, new information that was gleaned, how the exercises went, what worked, what didn't, and any issues that came up. Try to avoid making the discussion a counseling session unless you have a smaller, more intimate group with enough time for this. Questions are provided in the Leader's Guide for each day of the homework and can be used as a guideline to administer your group. They may be adapted to individual needs and experience levels.

The second segment should be spent introducing the new lesson and previewing the next week's homework (10 minutes). This would be considered teaching or instruction time and may involve advanced preparation on the part of the group leader. Discussion questions and content ideas are provided for each week, or you can be creative and develop your own.

Finally, close the class time with prayer, either corporately or with individual prayer requests (5-10 minutes). Again this would depend on the number of students. Some prayer ideas include assigning prayer partners to pray together, popcorn-style prayer, taking prayer requests from the front, or closing the class with a general prayer.

If you have extra time, you may want to consider allowing the groups to review how they applied the lessons in their marriage or discuss the concepts from the book or study.

Partner or Mentor-Directed Study

Doing this study with a partner or mentor is very effective. Select a mentor or a partner who would be willing to go through the materials with you. Each week or month a different chapter and exercise would need to be completed before the next meeting. When you meet, significant time should be spent describing what happened when you completed the exercises—like you would with an accountability partner. If the exercises were not completed, consider re-doing the same exercise until it is completed. It is crucial not to hurry through the material. It is more important that the material penetrates and changes thinking patterns to make a lasting difference.

You can initiate a mentor-directed study yourself by asking someone you respect or admire to mentor you through this study. Or, perhaps you can come alongside someone else as a mentor. Pray and ask the Lord to direct you to the right person. Acquire the materials, agree on the frequency, meeting dates, and location and submit the partnership to the Lord. Get ready to see what mighty works will be accomplished in both of your marriages.

Session 1—The First Day

1. **Administrative details:**
   Greet your students and distribute books. Have them fill out a registration form or sign-in sheet with their contact information and the best way to communicate with them. Allow a little extra time at the beginning of class to find a seat. For latecomers, you may want to recruit help for checking them in so you can focus on getting the class started in a timely manner. Nametags are helpful to learn names quickly and get familiar with each of them.

2. **Welcome and introduction:**
   Open the class in prayer. Take a few minutes to introduce yourself. Provide your contact information for questions and counsel throughout the study. You may want to talk about how you became interested in teaching *God's Radical Plan for Wives* and what they hope to learn during the class. Communicate the class goals:

   - *For women to radically change the way they think about their role in the marriage.*
   - *To increase the joy and intimacy of their marriage.*
   - *To understand and meet the needs of their husbands—needs that God designed them to have that only wives can meet.*
   - *To model and pass on the legacy of a healthy, joy-filled marriage to their children, family, and friends.*

3. **Getting to know you:**
   Take a few minutes to allow the women in the class (or within small groups of 6-8) to get acquainted with one another. Have them introduce themselves, talk about their families, a little bit about themselves, and (importantly) what they hope to learn from the class.

4. **Class format, guidelines, prayer time:**
   First Day: The first day will be a little different than the following weeks.
   Use this day to explain the weekly class format, how the class will operate, and how you will conduct prayer time. You can decide as a class if you want to provide beverages or a light snack to share.
   Future Sessions: A typical session will include a review of the previous week's homework; question and answer time; and discussion time within the groups, if possible. A short teaching of the topic for the next week will be presented, followed by prayer time.

5. **Workbooks and homework:**
   Walk through the workbook with the students, pointing out the introduction and the authors' pages. Each student will need a copy of the *God's Radical Plan for Wives* book by Gil & Dana Stieglitz, a copy of the *Companion Bible Study Workbook* by Jennifer Edwards, an easy-to-understand *Bible* (NIV, ESV, NASB), a dictionary (recommend on-line), and a journal (optional). Each day's homework can take anywhere from 30 minutes to an hour depending on how deep the student decides to go and how many of the application exercises she decides to do. The students will first read the passage in the book designated for each day and then complete the questions and exercises in the workbook. Each week will normally have five days of homework, however the first and last weeks only have three days. There

are a total of nine lessons, designed for completion over ten weeks. The tenth week is based on the "Conclusion" and is designed to be a wrap-up session.

Each day ends with the same question, "If I am to follow *God's Radical Plan for Wives,* I need to work on...." This acts as a prompt to get the student to think about practical things to work on in her marriage. At the end of each week, a page is provided to transfer her response for each day in the "Weekly Wrap-Up," ending with the question, "What is the **#1 take-a-way** you had from this week's lesson?" This will provide her a way to remember a specific point she learned and how it affected her thinking.

Each week the students will be given a "Mini-Assignment" to foster application. This can be assigned toward the end of class and reviewed at the beginning of the next class time. They are meant to be fun and interactive.

6. **Introduction teaching:**
Since the class won't have any homework to discuss this first week, the leader can begin introducing the background material located in the appendix and introductions of the books.
   - Introduce the authors of the books, why the materials were written, and what they are meant to achieve (see Introductions and Authors' pages of *God's Radical Plan for Wives* and the *Companion Bible Study Workbook*).
   - It would be beneficial to explain the chart on *The Five Problems of Marriage* featured in Dr. Stieglitz's book, *Marital Intelligence*. See Appendix 1 & 2.
   - Introduce the needs of men using the acrostic R.A.D.I.C.A.L. (Appendix 3) and briefly explain what the students can expect to learn about each category.
   - Introduce what a wife needs, using the acrostic H.U.S.B.A.N.D. (Appendix 4), which is developed in Dr. Stieglitz's book, *God's Radical Plan for Husbands.*
   - For more information, *Marital Intelligence* and *God's Radical Plan for Husbands* is available on hard copy and audio book formats at www.ptlb.com, and they are available on Kindle as well.

7. **Lesson 1:**
This week the students will read the Introduction, Chapter 1, "The Role of Wife," and Chapter 2, "Affecting Change" in *God's Radical Plan for Wives.* There will only be three days of homework this week; one day for each chapter. The homework questions flow with the reading. There isn't a "Mini-Assignment" assigned this first week.

8. **Close with prayer:**
Finally, close the class time with prayer, either corporately or with individual prayer requests (5-10 minutes). Again, this would depend on the number of students in the class and their comfort level for praying out loud. Some prayer ideas include assigning prayer partners to pray together, "popcorn" style prayer, taking prayer requests from the front, or closing the class with a general prayer. Invite the students to contact you privately for more confidential prayer requests if you feel comfortable. It is crucial to keep the confidentiality of the women in this class. That needs to be stressed over and over again.

9. **Follow-up and communication is critical:**
   Throughout the week, make contact with the ladies in the class. Let them know you are praying for them and rooting them on in their journey toward a healthy, joy-filled marriage. A nice card, e-mail message, text, or phone call works wonders to foster trust and show your care for them. Try to make yourself available to work through any issues they may have with the material throughout the week.

Session 2

1. **Open in prayer.**
2. **Greet and introduce new students to the group. (15 minutes)**
   Optional: Have each class member answer the following "Opener Question": "Share with the class one Fun Fact about yourself."
3. **Review Lesson 1 Homework—Introduction, Chapters 1 & 2 (50 minutes)**
   This is an opportunity to connect with the class and help them through any parts that were confusing or difficult. This may require breaking into smaller groups of 5-8 depending on the class size. Start with Day 1 and move on through each day's lesson, including anything they want to share from the reading and Marriage Exercises. You may use the discussion questions below as a guide to help you.

Lesson 1 Discussion Questions

Day 1
1. Was there anything from the reading that stood out to you?
2. (Q. 2) What do you think is at the heart of why the authors wrote this book?
3. (Q. 3) According to the reading, what does it mean to love someone? What do you think the author means by this?
4. (Q. 4) What can happen to a marriage when a wife begins to meet the deepest needs in her husband?
5. (Q. 5) Discuss the two pathways to marital bliss? Which one are you on?

Day 2
1. Was there anything from the reading that stood out to you?
2. (Q. 2-4) Discuss the roles women play. What ones are we most proud of? What ones are difficult? Why?
3. (Q. 5) How can a wife positively or negatively influence those around her?
4. (Q. 6) Discuss the people who have influenced the represented views of "wife."
5. (Q. 7) Discuss if there are any differences in the way they view or carry out the role from the way it was modeled to them or how they were taught.

Day 3
1. Was there anything from the reading that stood out to you?
2. (Q. 2) Discuss how whether a man's deepest relational needs are met, or not, influences his development as a man? How?
3. (Q. 3) Discuss the biblical definition of love from the reading. Does it just happen? How do emotions and feelings come into play?
4. (Q. 4-8) Discuss the dolphin experiment and if it can relate to getting your needs met? What are a husband's "fish"?
5. (Q. 9) How is a marriage like an organization? How might this affect the attitude of the husband and wife if they considered it this way?
6. (Q. 10) Like Dana, do you have examples of times when you appreciated things your husband did even if they didn't meet your standards? How could you do more of this?

Overall
Can anyone share their #1 take-a-way from this week's lesson?

4. **Lesson 2 Teaching Time—Chapter 3, Respect (10 minutes)**
   This is a time for teaching the first letter of the acrostic "R" which is "Respect." This need is often the most challenging for women to understand and put into practice, but it is very important to a man's life.
   - When you think of the word *respect,* what comes to mind? Brainstorm with the class.
   - What does it mean? A working definition is "to acknowledge value." It means to focus on a person's strengths, contributions, positions, accomplishments, and abilities.
   - What are some actions that typically demonstrate respect? Brainstorm.
   - What are some actions that typically demonstrate disrespect? Brainstorm.
   - What does one have to do to be treated with respect? It is to be earned or given freely?
   - In your Bible, let's look up a foundational verse for this lesson: Ephesians 5:33.
   "So again I say, 'Each man must love his wife as he loves himself, and the wife must respect her husband.'"
     - In the Greek, the word respect is the word "*phobetai,*" which comes from the word phobia or "fear of." It means that the person or object is of high value and one would be afraid to not give the proper value. This is not a terrorizing fear but rather a reverential fear—one of respect and awe.
     - This Scripture commands wives to place their husbands at such a high value that she should be afraid not to respect him! We are to place him in his proper place and attribute him his proper value.
     - Why do you think the Apostle Paul, who wrote Ephesians, commanded wives to respect their husbands? Paul wanted to make sure that all women understood the importance of valuing their husbands. Doing so will result in a stable, intimate marriage. Not doing so could result in your husband not meeting his potential, and possibly destroy the marriage.

5. **What to expect this week in the workbook:**
   The exercises in the workbook will take you through many passages in the Bible. We will even look up words in the dictionary to plumb the depths of this commandment! Days 1 & 2 will go into depth on *respect* and its full meaning. The remaining days will be more application focused—the *how* of respecting our husbands.

   Encourage them to do their homework and reading throughout the week but let them know that if it's too much to do, they should focus on the verses and definitions so they will be on the same page as the rest of the class in the discussion next week. Have them select a couple of the application exercises that sound appealing to them.

6. **Mini-Assignment:** Do *The Power of a Compliment* Marriage Exercise #1

7. **Prayer time.**

8. **Follow-up and communication.**

Session 3

1. **Open in prayer.**
2. **Greet and introduce new students to the group. (15 minutes)**
   * Optional: Have each class member answer the following "Opener Question": "When you think of the special man in your life, what are one or two things you consider to be "magical" about him?"
3. **Review Lesson 2 Homework, Respect (50 minutes)**
   Start with Day 1 and move on through each day's lesson, including anything they want to share from the reading and the Marriage Exercises. You may use the discussion questions below as a guide to help you.

Lesson 2 Discussion Questions

Day 1
1. (Q. 2, 3) When we read the story about Beth, what was the issue with her husband? What were some of her characteristics and traits? How did they make Dave feel about her?
2. (Q. 4) Let's look at the verses we looked up and see what they said about attitude and actions of a wife: Ephesians 5:33. Is respect a command or suggestion? Proverbs 12:4. What might a wife do to disgrace her husband? Proverbs 19:13. What does quarrelsome mean and how does it affect the husband?
3. (Q. 5) What is the definition of respect; what do you acknowledge?
   What are five positive ways to show your husband respect?
4. F, T, T, F, T, F
5. *Mini-Assignment: Power of a Compliment. Did anyone do one of the exercises? Share how it went with the class.*

Day 2
1. (Q. 2, 3) What are some sources in our lives that tell us we are valuable? What are the possible risks that come when respect is withheld?
2. (Q. 4) What did we learn from defining the words? Go through each one.
3. How did it expand your understanding of what respect looks like?
4. (Q. 6) What did you learn about the meanings of *father, mother & wife wound*?

Day 3
1. From the introduction on Day 3, what does respect give your husband?
2. (Q. 2-8) Is there anything you would like to share about these questions?
3. (Q. 9) What did you learn about refrain/avoidance?
4. (Q. 10, 11) Did you find out what spiritual gifts your husband has? Temperament?
5. Did you have a chance to go through the Accomplishments Inventory (ME#3)?

> **Day 4**
> 1. (Q. 2) What did we learn about expectations? How important are they?
> 2. (Q. 3) How do you know if expectations are unrealistic or not?
> 3. (Q. 4) Did you find anything enlightening to you as you looked at met needs vs. unmet needs?
> 4. T, T, F, T, F
> 5. (Q. 8) Did you find looking up the definitions useful? What new thing did you learn?
> 6. (Q. 9) What were some of the positive responses you came up with for each one?
>
> **Day 5**
> 1. (Q. 2) We learned that men receive respect in different ways. What are they?
> 2. (Q. 3, 4) Share your husband's type. What were three things you could do to make sure he receives your message of respect?
> 3. (Q. 5) How important is establishing and keeping boundaries in a relationship?
>
> **Overall**
> Can anyone share their #1 take-a-way from this week's lesson?

4. **Lesson 3 Teaching—Chapter 4, Adapt (10 minutes)**
   This is a time for teaching the second letter of the acrostic R.A.D.I.C.A.L,
   "A," adapt. In the dictionary "to adapt" means: *"To make fit for, or change to suit a new purpose; to make suitable to requirements or conditions; adjust or modify fittingly."*

   ### Think of adapting as making music:
   A marriage is like making music. It can be a harmonious team – like a symphony orchestra – where everyone works together creating beautiful music. Some instruments play the main chorus, while others play the harmony. Of course, if the musicians decided to do things their own way, what would happen? What music would be made if the clarinets decided they wanted to play the music of the kettledrum or the brass instruments the notes of the woodwinds? It would sound terrible! Not to mention that in doing so, the musicians would be going directly against the conductor, which is never a good idea! (In the case of marriage, can you guess who the conductor is?)

   Just like an orchestra, you and your husband can create a symphony of beautiful music together for the world to enjoy. Believe it or not, people are watching your performance! When you work together, it is GOOD! But if one of you insists on playing to his or her own tune and not blending the notes to those the other plays, then your orchestra plays a *cacophony* and is painful to all who hear it. If we aim to get our own way, then the music will be lousy.

   It's very likely that earlier in the relationship you and your husband adapted together. Think back to when you were dating—inevitably you found yourself making concessions like going to events you would have never considered before, listening to topics that bore you now, agreeing with his arguments, laughing at his jokes, or making allowances for peculiarities. But <u>after</u> marriage, somewhere between week two and year two, the natural adaptation begins to wear off. You may have witnessed his weaknesses, his inabilities, or found him irritating and helpless by now!

In this lesson you will:
- Learn to adapt to your true man and NOT the man you have set up in your mind or the man you think your husband ought to be like.
- Learn how each other's strengths can make up for the weaknesses in the other and find ways to work together to be healthy and productive.
- Figure out how to make the other person successful and what your part in that process entails.
- Put away the idea, "I shouldn't have to do this or that," or "HE should be doing this or that."
- Learn the true meaning and intention of *biblical submission*. It is the wise woman who seeks to understand biblical submission and put it into practice in her marriage. Proverbs 14:1 says, *"The wise woman builds her house, but with her own hands the foolish one tears hers down."*

5. **What to expect this week in the homework.**
This week's homework could be challenging for some. It can be lengthy in places, but it is very foundational and should be completed if possible. Day 1 will delve into relational peace and what it means to adapt or complement your husband. You'll also take an assessment of strengths and weaknesses. Days 2 & 3 will go into depth on *how you were designed to complement* your husband. You'll look up Bible verses and words in the dictionary. Days 4 & 5 are more application focused, dealing with his work and leadership.

Encourage your students to do their homework and reading throughout the week but let them know that if it's too much to do, they should focus on the verses and definitions so they will be on the same page as the rest of the class in the discussion next week. This is a very meaty and useful week of homework if they can do it all. Have them select a couple of the application exercises that sound appealing to them.

6. **Mini-Assignment.**
This week, have the class practice deferring to their husbands by allowing him to choose which restaurant to eat at or which activity he wants to do without complaint or arguing from her. She should simply defer to his choice. If the couple is going out to eat, the wife should even allow the husband to order for her! In fact, she should close the menu and suggest he make the decision. She should determine to be grateful and happy with whatever he chooses, knowing she is honoring and respecting him and allowing him to think of her in a new way. Say, "Honey, you choose where we go tonight," and "How about you order for me? You know what I like. Whatever you choose for me is fine." They should be ready to share their experiences with the class next week.

7. **Prayer time.**

8. **Follow-up and communication.**

Session 4

1. **Open in prayer.**

2. **Greeting, Review Mini-Assignment (15 minutes)**
   Did you have a chance to defer to your husband in choosing a restaurant? Did you allow him to order for you? What was his response? How did it go?

3. **Review Lesson 3 Homework, Adapt (50 minutes)**

> ### Lesson 3 Discussion Questions
>
> **Day 1**
> 1. (Q. 2) Did anyone relate to Shelia, the woman in the story? How?
> 2. (Q. 3) What new thoughts came out when you defined the words "adapt," "compliment," and "accept"?
> 3. (Q. 4-5) How did looking up "dynamic," "harmony," "cacophony," and "peace" help you understand the peace in a marriage relationship? What are some things you wrote down about how you would like your marriage to be?
> 4. F, T, F, T, T
> 5. (Q. 7-10) When you did the His & Hers outline, did you find any areas that complemented each other? Could you see how your strengths make up for his weaknesses and vice versa?
> 6. (Q. 11-13) What do you think it means to adapt in terms of marriage? What are some ways you can change in order to help make him successful and have a great marriage?
>
> **Day 2**
> 1. Talk about what you learned regarding biblical submission and how it differs from the culture's idea of submission.
> 2. (Q. 2-5) What did you learn from the verses we looked up? What were some things that stood out to you?
> 3. (Q. 6) Discuss the meanings of the words.
> 4. (Q. 7-11) Discuss what you learned about "hupotasso" and some of the advantages in marriage.
>
> **Day 3**
> 1. (Q. 1) What did you learn from the verses we looked up? What were some things that stood out to you?
> 2. (Q. 2) Talk about what you learned about "suitable helper."
> 3. (Q. 3) Why is submission so difficult? What did we learn?
> 4. (Q. 4) What did you learn about the 5 W's & an H of submission?
> 5. After doing this lesson, do you have a better understanding of biblical submission than before this lesson? On a scale of 1 to 5, give your rating. What is still missing for you? What makes more sense to you? What has been your response to what you learned?

> **Day 4**
> 1. (Q. 2) Discuss expectations and how they can get in the way of adapting to the man we really married.
> 2. (Q. 3) Discuss comparison and how it can impact how we feel about our husbands.
> 3. (Q. 4-6) Answer the questions from the homework.
> 4. (Q. 7-8) How can we adapt to our husbands ideas?
> 5. (Q. 9-17) What did we learn about "work" in this lesson?
> 6. How important is work to a man?
> 7. Are there things you do that might hinder your husband in his work, or make it hard for him to realize God's plan for him and his work?
> 8. What are some positive things you currently do or are going to do to help him with his work life?
>
> **Day 5**
> 1. (Q. 2) What are the two myths in regard to leadership in marriage?
> 2. T, F, F, T, T, F, T
> 3. (Q. 4-7) Leadership in the home.
> 4. (Q. 8-10) How have you adapted to his personality/temperaments?
> 5. (Q. 11-12) His phobias? How can you help him with this?
> 6. (Q. 13) Adapting to his background and experiences.
> 7. (Q. 14) Adapting to his culture or heritage.
> 8. (Q. 15) Are there any questions on over-adapting? What does it mean?
>
> **Overall**
> Can anyone share their #1 take-a-way from this week's lesson?

4. **Lesson 4 Teaching—Chapter 5, Domestic Leadership (10 minutes)**
   This is a time for teaching the third letter of the acrostic R.A.D.I.C.A.L, "D," which is *Domestic Leadership*.
   - What comes to mind when you think of the term *Domestic Leadership*?

   - Does it imply only basic household chores?

   - Who does this phrase apply to?

   - Does it only apply to the wife who "stays at home"?

   - What if you work full-time outside the home?

   - What feelings or emotions does it conjure up?

   - What stigmas are attached to this idea?

   - Does it make a difference knowing that this particular area is a place of tremendous impact where wives and mothers make the greatest difference in the lives of family members? Let's see how.

"Home" Defined

The concept of "HOME" is more than just bricks and mortar; more than the physical building we live in. *Smithsonian Magazine* has a great article about the idea of home with this quote: *"Be it ever so humble, it's more than just a place. It's also an idea—one where the heart is."* Here are some other quotes about "home" to share:

Charity begins at home. (1 Timothy 5:4)
"When the pressures of the world intrude, there is no shelter like a peaceful home."
"Home is where the heart is." – Pliny the Elder
"Home interprets heaven. Home is heaven for beginners." – Charles Henry Parkhurst
A poem by Lena Guilbert Ford ~ *Keep the Home Fires Burning, 1915*

> *Keep the home fires burning,*
> *While your hearts are yearning;*
> *Though your lads are far away*
> *They dream of coming home.*
> *There's a silver lining*
> *Through the dark cloud shining;*
> *Turn the dark cloud inside out,*
> *Till the boys come home.*

The *"Heart of the Home"* is the very essence of that place where our families come home to everyday. As women and wives, we have a tremendous impact on making a home either a good, beneficial impact or a bad, negative one. As the domestic leader of our homes, we get to shape the very nature of "home" in the hearts and minds of our kids and husbands. We, my friends, are the heartbeat!

As you go through this week's lesson, you will learn about the need for peace at home and our God-given responsibilities as wives. You will see that we have a bigger, more important job than we realize. It's awesome how God must really trust us since he gave us responsibility over so much!

You'll also be introduced to a new term, *the Oikodespotein*, and what it means fully to be a wise "house leader." Anyone can be a house leader, but what does it take to be one that is wise and godly?

You will learn how to meet this need for a man and why the need is so great. You'll glean answers to questions like, "Why does it mean so much to them?" "What impact does it have in all areas of his life?" "What can a wife do to make sure he keeps coming home?" "What happens when she chooses to downplay or ignore this role?" "How does this fit in with the *overall leadership* of the home/marriage?" "Does this mean she has to do everything herself?" and "How will she manage it all?"

5. **What to expect this week in the homework.**

Again, this week's homework could be challenging for some. It may be challenging for women in the work force, but the reading and homework address the issue. Day 1 will delve into the need for peace at home. Students will be asked to create a vision for their home and brainstorm changes to realize the vision. Day 2 covers the concept of the "Oikodespotein" and we will explore the biblical insight about this. Day 3 teaches on the "Heart of the Home" and Days 4 & 5 explore male and female differences, providing exercises to help students develop a plan.

Encourage your students to do their homework and reading throughout the week, but let them know that if it's too much to do, they should focus on the verses and definitions so they will be on the same page as the rest of the class in the discussion next week. Have them select a couple of the application exercises that sound appealing to them

6. **Mini-assignment:** This week, students are to ask their husbands the question, *"Honey, is there anything I can help you with today?"* Ideally, they would ask this question every day. The husband may not take her seriously the first time and might not be prepared with an answer the first time. She should try again until he comes up with something tangible. She should be prepared to share her experience next week!

7. **Prayer time.**

8. **Follow-up and communication.**

Session 5

1. **Open in prayer.**
2. **Greeting, Review Mini-Assignment (15 minutes)**
   Did you ask your husband the question, "Honey, is there anything I can help you with today?" How did it go? How did he react? What did he ask you to do? Did you notice any positive effects afterwards? How have you done at meeting his need for respect and adaption this week?

3. **Review Lesson 4 Homework—Domestic Leadership (50 minutes)**

Lesson 4 Discussion Questions

Day 1
1. (Q. 2) From the story of Bill and Sally, what was Bill's need in the home? What did Bill need Sally to do? Was he being reasonable? Why or why not?
2. (Q. 3) What definition of the word "peace" did you discover?
3. (Q. 4) Share about how your home compares to the home you would like it to be?
4. (Q. 5) What are "Peace Busters" and do you have any of them in your home?
5. (Q. 6) What are tangible things to do to make your home the way you want it to be?

Day 2
1. In Bible times, the wife of the household was deemed as highly important, a valued leader in the family life. The book described the home as the *"place of business, learning, security, and success—the center out of which all of life operated for the family."* Is this outdated? Does it still apply to today's modern family?
2. (Q. 2) What did we learn about "oikourgos" and "oikodespotein"?
3. (Q. 3-5) Discuss Titus 2:3-5 and 1Timothy 5:14. What do they tell women to do? What was the general reason given to be workers at home for both of these verses?
4. (Q. 6) What did you learn about how and why a wife who doesn't keep her home in order could dishonor God? What is at stake?
5. (Q. 7-9) Do you agree or disagree with this statement? *"The home is not the only place where a woman can direct her energy, but it is the number one priority."* Will you make any changes in your priorities?" Why or why not?
6. (Q. 10-12) Since a wife is vital to the development of a great marriage and family, what adjustments need to be made?
8. (Q. 13-14) If you are a working wife, how do you and your husband handle the domestic arena? Are you a team? Do you share in the duties? Is there balance?
9. (Q. 15-16) Discuss the symptoms of a needed change.

> **Day 3**
> 1. (Q. 2) Review the Bible verses and explain what God says about the role of a wife in the home.
> 2. T, F, F, T, T
> 3. (Q. 3, 4) What are some of the skills and abilities needed to manage and lead a household?
> 4. (Q. 4) Does anyone want to share some of the positive traits that you identified about yourself? How about any of the negative traits?
>
> **Day 4**
> 1. (Q. 2, 3) What are some risks of not taking the domestic leadership role seriously?
> 2. (Q. 4, 5) What are some differences in the way men and women view the home? What differences are there between you and your husband?
> 3. (Q. 6-7) What did you learn from reading Proverbs 31:10-31? What did you learn about the words you looked up?
> 4. (Q. 8) Does anyone want to share the paragraph they wrote about a wife who is considered "wise?"
>
> **Day 5**
> 1. (Q. 2) Do husbands play a role in the details of the home? What? How?
> 2. (Q. 3) How do you and your husband share in planning or problem solving in the home? Is this working or not? How can it change for the good?
> 3. (Q. 4) Do you have anything to share in this exercise? Was this helpful to you? What did you find out about your strengths and weaknesses? What are you going to do about weak areas?
> 4. If there is time, review Marriage Exercise #5.
>
> **Overall**
> Can anyone share their #1 take-a-way from this week's lesson?

4. **Lesson 5 Teaching—Chapter 6, Intimacy (20 minutes)**
   The "low-down" on marital intimacy:
   - God wired both men and women to need physical contact – just in different ways. Women need a tender touch and displays of affection. Men need sexual contact and are physiologically wired to need sexual climax every few days (2-5 days). Sexual release actually provides the ENERGY a man needs to be able to do the things he is called to do, including loving his wife the way he is called to do. Women typically only need a sexual release about once a month, usually based on her highest fertility point in her cycle. Once a woman is done with being fertile and her body goes through "the change," her desire tends to goes way down—but this is not an excuse to withdraw sexually from her husband.
   - The need for intimacy in men is more complicated than just physical release. Intimacy is a man's way of connecting emotionally, spiritually, and relationally to his wife. Their whole being gets wrapped up in intimacy and there is only one woman in the world that can meet it without guilt—his wife.

- The need for sexual intimacy in a man is intense and constant. In fact, it is nearly impossible for him to focus on other aspects of his marriage and family when this need is constantly screaming at him! As women we cannot possibly relate, but perhaps we can think about how annoying or distracting it is when you have a child that won't stop talking or crying! Or, an itch that won't go away. But then tie into emotions of rejection and feelings of being unloved and maybe then it would come close to how a man might feel. What if a baby continued to cry and instead of it being just an annoying distraction, you actually felt, "The baby won't stop crying so it must not love me. I must not be good enough for him/her." Or, "I can't get this itch to go away and there is only one person who can scratch it, but she refuses. She must not care."

What do husbands need from their wives?
- He needs you to want him sexually. They have fragile egos and can easily take your "no" to mean you don't love him or aren't attracted to him.
- He needs you to want and enjoy physical intimacy yourself—for you to engage.
- He needs a wife who identifies the tension building up in him and wants to help him release it (by learning his sexual cycle).
- He needs a wife who will "listen" to his soul during physical intimacy. This is the way to get him to open up about his thoughts, feelings, dreams, and also how you begin educating him about how to meet your needs.

A Wise, "Godly Wife" Strategy—Love him first.
Just as a woman is drawn to her man when he gives her honor, understanding, and affection, a man is drawn to his wife when his number one need is met—sexual intimacy. If we demand the other to love us first before we love them, usually there is a stand-off and a great deal of sexual tension. This really says, "I will love you if you earn my love" and is the opposite of unconditional love. God FIRST loved us so we could love Him, so in the same way we can submit to the idea that if we choose to love our husbands first, then he will meet our needs. Since he cannot read our minds, wives will have to remember to gently and lovingly communicate those to him.

Let me read you a note from the author:

Author's Note
"It's quite possible that God put this constant physiological need in men so they would be constantly drawn back to their wives. A man is never far from the pull of this need, and it causes his mind, emotions, and body to constantly be turned toward home. If home is the place where this relentless need is lovingly and tenderly met in his life, he will be more open to the wisdom, correction, and development his wife can offer him. He desperately needs the woman he married. Every few days, his entire focus is directed toward you to satisfy the longing of his mind, soul, and body. **He is tethered to you if he is to live free from guilt.**

I believe God did this because a man has a natural orientation toward self-sufficiency and new worlds to conquer. If there were not an internal mechanism that directed him back to his wife and family, he would mentally, emotionally, and spiritually move away from them, seeking his fulfillment, fame, and success completely apart from them. Unfortunately, because of relaxing sexual rules and mores in our society, this is what's happening. Men are finding ways outside their marriage to satisfy their sexual needs. They are not taught tenderness, faithfulness, and real love by relating to their wives. Men who can have their sexual needs met through casual sex with strangers become more selfish, aggressive, and rapacious in all the dealings of their lives.

A wife's understanding of her husband's sexual cycle will help him avoid the ravages of anonymous sex or pornography."— Gil Stieglitz

5. **What to expect this week in the homework.**
   - We are going to look at what the Bible says about "becoming one flesh" and how we can help meet the number one need of our spouse.
   - We will look at the way men and women are hardwired for intimacy.
   - We will learn more godly wife strategies to meet this need.
   - You will determine your husband's sexual cycle and how to recognize the signs.
   - We will also deal with our role as wives in trying to prevent our husbands from sexual immorality and pornography and will discuss setting boundaries.

6. **Mini-Assignment:** This week's mini-assignment is for each married woman to figure out the sexual cycle of her husband. There is no need to share this information with the class–it's between the two of them.

7. **Prayer time.**

8. **Follow-up and communication.**

Session 6

1. **Open in prayer.**

2. **Greeting, Review Mini-Assignment** (15 minutes)
   Finding out about your husband's sexual cycle: how did it go? Were there any surprises? Was it easy to figure out? How does knowing it affect your thinking about his sexual needs?

3. **Review of Lesson 5 Homework—Chapter 6, Intimacy** (50 minutes)

Lesson 5 Discussion Questions

Day 1
1. (Q. 2) Review the definition of *intimacy* and its synonyms.
2. (Q. 3) Review 1 Corinthians 7:1-5. Go through each question.
3. (Q. 4) Review Genesis 2:24 and Matthew 19:4-6. Answer each question.
4. (Q. 5) What are the differences for men and women sexually?
5. F, T, T, F, T, F
6. (Q. 7) Review the various types of sexual intimacy.
7. (Q. 8-9) Discuss the risks of not meeting the sexual need. Privacy and confidentiality is important here.
8. (Q. 10) How does a woman's own sexual self-image affect intimacy?
9. Discuss Marriage Exercise #1.

Day 2
1. (Q. 2) According to 1 John 4:19, can we decide to love first? Why should we?
2. (Q. 3) What do the verses say about applying the principle of loving him first?
3. Is it always the case that men desire sex more than women? If not, what can the woman do?
4. (Q. 4) Discuss the points they marked with a check. Were any of them new thoughts?
5. (Q. 5) What are signs and symptoms that he is needy?
6. (Q. 6) Sexual cycle—discuss any questions.

Day 3
1. (Q. 2) Discuss responses to the reading passage.
2. (Q. 3) How does your life stage affect intimacy and sexual expression? Older couples? Young children? Illness?
3. (Q. 4-13) Is there anything from these questions you would like to share or discuss? They are mostly application questions and privacy is important.
4. (Q. 14) What are four ways your husband will be able to receive new information sexually?
5. Marriage Exercise #2: Did anyone try the three-day challenge?

> **Day 4**
> 1. (Q. 2) Review Hebrews 13:4 and Ephesians 5:3. What do they say?
> 2. (Q. 3) What did you find out by looking up the definitions?
> 3. (Q. 4) What did you find in 1 Corinthians 6:12-20 about sexual immorality?
> 4. (Q. 5) Is there anything in these questions you would like to share or discuss?
> 5. (Q. 6-7) What types of boundaries should there be in sexual intimacy?
> 6. (Q. 8-10) Review Matthew 5:27-28. Does this verse impact your understanding of whether viewing pornography would be considered marital unfaithfulness or not?
> 7. (Q. 11) How can a wife help her husband refrain or have the strength to withstand temptations? *Remind her that she is not responsible for his sin, but she can help him have the energy he needs to overcome temptation.*
> 8. If she feels her husband is caught up in pornography, it is important to get educated about the problem and have compassion toward him. Some resources we can recommend:
>   - *Hope After Betrayal* by Meg Wilson
>   - *Affair of the Mind* by Laurie Hall
>   - *Mission Possible* by Gil Stieglitz
>   - *Every Man's Battle* by Stephen Artreburn
>   - *Every Heart Restored* by Fred & Brenda Stoeker
>   - www.marriagemissions.com
>
> **Day 5**
> 1. (Q. 2) What are four intimate ways that show him you love him?
> 2. F, T, T, F, T, F, T, T, T, F
> 3. (Q. 4-6) Initiating and signaling intimacy—any questions?
>
> **Overall**
> Can anyone share their #1 take-a-way from this week's lesson?

4. **Introduction of Lesson 6—Chapter 7, Companionship** (10 minutes)

   "It is not good for the man to be alone." Genesis 2:18

   God made man to need companionship in his life. One of the main reasons a man gets married is for companionship. He wants someone to share his life with who really enjoys his interests, pursuits, careers, and ideas. This need for companionship ranks high next to physical intimacy and respect. The godly wife understands his need for companionship and seeks to love him by meeting that need in the best way she can. This week we will explore what side-by-side love is. This type of love is about enjoying common interests and activities. The key is to find something he likes to do and do it with him. To have a great marriage, this is a requirement, not an option.

When you were dating, you might have faked interest to win him over. But after marriage, the interest may have dwindled somewhat. If you really think about it, it's a form of "false advertising" since men select their spouse by her willingness to engage in activities they both like! If a wife becomes self-focused and engages exclusively on those activities and hobbies she is most interested in, she opens a chasm between them. It's not that she can't have her own interests, she just needs to make sure to leave enough room in her life for interests that they both share.

The secret to being a good companion to your husband is to perfect how he needs you to be his friend in the various parts of his life. Finding activities you both enjoy together and supporting the activities he's involved with will significantly improve your marriage. The circumstances of your life may preclude you from being as involved as both of you would like but be creative and don't give up! Try to find what works best for both of you.

This lesson may seem pretty basic to you; but we can easily forget that husbands and wives need to be friends, not just parents and mates. When we don't foster our friendship with one another, our whole marriage suffers and can fall apart once the kids are gone.

5. **What to expect this week in the homework.**
This week's lesson will help you understand what men gain from companionship and how God addresses this need. You'll learn what true companionship and friendship means and, how as a wife, you can fill that need in the way your husband needs it. This week's marriage exercises are reflective and are designed to include your spouse, if possible.

6. **Mini-Assignment:**
How will you be his companion this week? Be prepared to share one way you spent time with your husband doing something he likes to do?

7. **Prayer time.**

8. **Follow-up and communication.**

Session 7

1. **Open in prayer.**
2. **Greeting, Review Mini-Assignment** (15 minutes)
   How were you your husband's companion this week? What was one way you spent time with your husband doing something he likes to do?
3. **Recap of Past Lessons** (10 minutes)
   - **Respect**—What did you learn about *respect* and how that applies to being a godly wife and loving your husband? Why do you think it was a command? What does a wife who shows respect to her husband communicate to him? (value, worth) If showing respect brings out positive things in your husband, what are some negatives things that can result if you don't show him respect?
   - **Adaptation**—What does it mean to adapt to your husband? How can marriage be like an orchestra? (Cacophony or symphony—describe each). What did you learn about submission? How can you adapt to him in life? Can you over-adapt?
   - **Domestic Leadership**—What is the oikodespotein? Is she honorable? What are some of her characteristics? Why is a wife's role of leading on the home front important? Does working outside the home negate the responsibility? How can a working mom sort this out?
   - **Intimacy**—Why is a man's need for intimacy so strong? Regarding sexual intimacy, why is it important for wives to be willing to meet the need as often as his cycle requires? What are risks of not meeting this need? What are other ways to express intimacy? Is there anything from last week that you would like to address?

4. **Review Lesson 6 Homework—Chapter 7, Companionship** (50 min.)

Lesson 6 Discussion Questions

Day 1
1. (Q. 2) Review the story of Kelly and Steve. They were unmarried, but how would this have been different if they were married?
2. (Q. 3) Why do men like the recreational pursuits they do? How do they fulfill him?
3. (Q. 4) What two things does a man gain from his companions?
4. (Q. 5) What is God asking wives to do?
5. (Q. 6) What will wives have if they are good companions to their husbands?
6. (Q. 7) What are three main risks you take as a wife when you don't engage in the activities and interests of your husband? What can be done to minimize them?
7. (Q. 8) Is it intuitive for wives to know how to be a friend to their husband?
8. (Q. 9) What does side-by-side love mean? How is it working in your marriage?
9. (Q. 10) Definitions: Companion, Accompany, Soul Mate, Fellowship, and Friend. How do they pertain to marital relationships?
10. (Q. 11) How have you put this "companionship love" into practice?

Day 2
1. (Q. 2) Review the verses. What makes a good friend, what is the purpose of a friend, and what can separate them?
2. (Q. 3, 4) What should you do and not do to be a good friend to your husband?
3. (Q. 5) Discuss the first three points of understanding friendship?
4. (Q. 6-8) Did you take the time to go through these either on your own or with your spouse? Was it helpful? Anything of interest?

Day 3
1. (Q.2) Discuss the remaining three points of understanding friendship?
2. (Q. 3-5) Review the Bible verses: What did we learn about trials? Is this true for marriage?
3. (Q. 6) Can you share a struggle that you and your husband have been through and how it has impacted your marriage?
4. (Q. 7-12) Reviewing Common Memories—did anyone take the time to do this? This is a great journaling exercise and also really great to do when you are discouraged or down.
5. (Q. 13-14) Can you share how to get in time to talk and share with your husband? What is working, what isn't? Challenges?

Day 4
1. F, F, F, T, T
2. (Q. 3) Discuss the four types of companionship.
3. (Q. 4) Review the descriptions.
4. (Q. 5, 6) What kind of companion does your husband need you to be? How do you know? Are you meeting this need?

Day 5
1. (Q. 2) Review the Bible verses. What do they say to do or not to do regarding friendships?
2. (Q. 3) When is it okay not to participate in an activity with your husband?
3. (Q. 4) When you have determined that you cannot participate in an activity with your husband, what are the best steps to take?
4. F, T, T, F, T
5. (Q. 6-7) What are some of the great qualities of women you admire that make them a good friend? Why are these women a good friend for you?
6. (Q. 8-9) Write down any traits or attributes that would cause friendships to be "risky" to you.
7. (Q. 10-12) Review Philippians 2:14-15 and Titus 2:3-5. Answer the questions.

Overall
Can anyone share their #1 take-a-way from this week's lesson?

5. **Introduction of Lesson 7—Chapter 8, Attractive Body & Soul** (10 min.)

In the book, we meet Rachel. Rachel has a plain physical appearance. She worked hard on her physical appearance by working out, using some makeup, and wearing attractive clothes; but it was her soul that outshone the skin-deep beauty of other women. Her husband was captivated! Why? Because she always had a quick smile and warm greeting. She was almost manic in her ability to listen and express interest in others ideas, topics, and opinions; and she found reasons to be grateful and ways to be flexible. She was always positive and knew she served a great God who would work things out. Contrast that with a woman who is outwardly beautiful, yet is cold, calculating, ungrateful, bitter, jealous, demanding, and contentious. No one is drawn to that woman for very long.

We will look in-depth at two attractive soul qualities – gentleness and a quiet spirit. A woman with gentleness can be characterized as someone who has a readiness to adapt and adjust one's expectations to God's will and to others' needs. It is a willingness to lower your expectations of how the people in your family will act or be like, or perhaps what the perfect vacation will be, or how a celebration should be done.

Her main characteristic is "flexibility," especially in how she handles how others fail to meet her expectations. A rigid or excessively high expectation almost always leads to anger or some expression of selfishness. Anger is the by-product of unreasonable or unmet expectations. Inflexibility actually repels people. As women seeking gentleness, we need to learn to adjust our expectations with minimal pouting, demands, anger, and whining. Instead, we strive to react with grace and understanding when our expectations are not met.

A woman with a quiet spirit demonstrates this quality to others when she doesn't exacerbate a situation but instead brings a calm to it. When a wife acts as a sponge to dampen the fires of emotion and argumentation, she becomes very attractive to her husband. A wife who fosters calm and harmony in the midst of the storm is a remarkably beautiful woman.

We will also discuss outward beauty. Is it important? We will see what the Apostle Peter says about it in Scripture. Even though our outward beauty will fade, as long as our inward soul is beautiful, we will continue to be attractive to our men. This does not mean we shouldn't try to keep up our physical appearances, but long-term attractiveness is found in a beautiful soul. In fact, a symptom of a rotting soul is one who no longer cares about their physical appearance. I know that can be hard to hear; but it is possible that some women have given into the impulses of selfishness, laziness, pride, and envy, which leads to the fading of their outward beauty.

Ask yourself these questions:
- Does he enjoy being with you or does he avoid you?
- Does spending time with you cause him to forget his problems? Or do you remind him of them?
- Does spending time with you cause him to look at the world with a positive glow or to give the world a more pessimistic slant?
- Do you praise him and uplift him? Or do you feel the need to correct him constantly?

- Do you thank him for all that he's done? Or complain about what he has done or hasn't done?
- Can he count on you to be patient and gentle or to nag and be demanding?
- Are you frugal with the money he brings home? Or do you find ways to drain the bank account?

Key Point:

The godly wife doesn't spend huge amounts of time, energy, and money on her outward appearance but does enough to stay healthy and feel good about herself. Instead she focuses on her inward beauty, her heart, so she can do good works and bring glory to God. That leads to the more sustainable, long-term beauty we are seeking.

6. **What to expect this week in the homework.**

   This week we will cover five beauty secrets for the godly woman. We will look in depth at what true beauty really is and what it isn't. You'll learn how important it is to cultivate and balance internal and external beauty. You will delve into the core of a woman who attracts and one who repels, with biblical studies on the gentle and quiet spirit. And finally, we'll look at physical beauty and examine motivations for remaining attractive for our husbands and the risks of letting ourselves go physically. As usual, there will be plenty of application and reflective exercises to complete.

7. **Mini-assignment**

   The assignment is for each woman to treat herself to something good for her – whether it's a nap, a manicure, or a walk. She should be prepared to share what she did with the group next week.

8. **Prayer time.**

9. **Follow-up and communication.**

Session 8

1. **Open in prayer.**

2. **Greeting, Review Mini-Assignment** (15 minutes)
   How were you good to yourself this week? Did you treat yourself to something good for you? Share with the group.

3. **Review Lesson 7 Homework—Ch. 8, Attractive Soul/Body (50 min.)**

Lesson 7 Discussion Questions

Day 1
1. (Q. 2-4) Review the stories of Rachel and Isabel. What were some of the words that described these women? What is the key component of an attractive soul?
2. (Q. 5) Review 1 Peter 3:3-4. What does this verse say to us? *The Message's* version actually used the word "cultivate." What is the meaning of that word and its synonyms? What do they tell you about inner beauty? What does it require?
3. F, T, F, F, T, T, T
4. (Q. 7) Review the nine aspects of a woman with inner beauty in Marriage Exercises #1. Let's walk through these nine aspects and tell me if you can relate to any of them.
5. (Q. 8) What does it mean to create a "win" for your husband?
6. (Q. 9) What are three things a beautiful soul is not?
7. (Q. 10) What are some risks of not cultivating a beautiful soul?

Day 2
1. (Q. 2) What did we learn about one who attracts? What is the definitions of the words we looked up?
2. (Q. 3) Review 1 Peter 3:1-6. What are five traits that characterize an attractive wife? Review Proverbs 14:1; Proverbs 16:24; Proverbs 12:4. What does "noble character" mean? What does "her husband's crown" mean?
3. (Q. 4) Proverbs 31:10-31. Did anyone do this question? If so, how was she attractive?
4. (Q. 5) What did we learn about the one who repels? The definitions?
5. (Q. 6) Review the Bible verses: Proverbs 12:4b; Proverbs 21:9; Proverbs 21:19; Proverbs 27:15-16. What do they say about a "repellant" wife?
6. Marriage Exercise #1. Was this helpful to you to find areas where you might need to become more attractive vs. repellant?

Day 3
1. (Q. 2) What did you learn about *gentle*? What words describe it?
2. T, F, T, F, F, T, T, T
3. (Q. 4) Review 1 Peter 3:1-6 in the NASB version. Answer the questions.
4. (Q. 5) Is gentleness and a quiet spirit something we are born with? What does adorn mean?
5. (Q. 6) Why is having a gentle and quiet spirit important to God?

Day 4
1. (Q. 2) What did you learn about the *quiet spirit*? What words describe it?
2. T, F, F, T, F, F, T, T, T, F
3. (Q. 4-6) What does having a quiet spirit mean? What do you receive from people who have biblical, quiet spirits? Why does a person with a quiet spirit attract others to her?
4. (Q. 7) Can you think of someone in your life with a quiet spirit? How have they impacted your life?
5. (Q. 8) Why might a woman with a quiet spirit be more attractive to her husband? (Q. 5)
6. (Q. 9) Review the scenarios.
7. (Q. 10) What are ways you can cultivate these traits in yourselves?

Day 5
1. (Q. 2) From the reading, was there anything that stood out to you?
2. (Q. 3-5) What does physical attractive mean? Answer all questions.
3. (Q. 6-7) Review the Bible verses. How do they pertain to our bodies?
4. T, T, T, F, T, F, F, F, T, T
5. (Q. 9-10) Is modesty important? Why?
6. (Q. 11-12) Did you do the application exercises? Are there any changes you plan to make?

A few key points:
- To keep a great marriage intact, you must act like you are still trying to win his heart.
- If a woman is not willing to work on her side of the marriage, she is not in a position to leverage change in her husband.
- When we don't make an effort to be attractive for our husbands, they think, "If you do not appear interested in attracting or impressing me when we are together, you do not love me."

Overall
Can anyone share their #1 take-a-way from this week's lesson?

4. **Introduction of Lesson 8, Listening (10 minutes)**

Listening to your husband is critical.
Our husbands have the need for someone to listen to them and we are the ones to do it! In fact, this need is so deep that they may be tempted to betray all they hold dear just to have someone in their lives that will listen to them. This is the place where we can access our husband's very soul if we are willing to put aside some time and energy each day. We would do well to consider it a part of our ministry to them as their wives.

Listening is a skill to be mastered.
We'll employ our two beautiful soul traits that we learned from the last lesson—gentleness and a quiet spirit—to provide this need of listening for them. We will learn what it means to listen in an active-detached manner. It takes a strong resolve to not react to his emotions while he is talking. Just by allowing him to feel and talk about things without demanding a response, you are fulfilling his need to be listened to. Being unemotional and calm during this process – especially when he is telling you how he'd like to move the family, quit his job, kill his boss, etc. – can be extremely challenging. But this is what we are to do; it is a critical part of the listening process.

To carry out this role, you have to put your trust, focus, and security in God. It's the only way you can prepare to hear things that you would naturally react to in anger, repulsion, and fear. You are to listen with *active detachment*. If you don't learn to listen this way, he will come to realize you are not a safe person to open up to and will find someone else to talk to. He is looking for someone safe enough to hear it and not jump to conclusions that he would actually act on his impulses. He needs someone who can hear all about who he is, his insecurities, his fears, his fantasies, his dreams, scars, and so on.
You'll do this by:
- *Staying on his topic;*
- *Asking questions;*
- *Providing insights;*
- *Letting him talk;*
- *Reflecting back what he seems to be feeling and thinking.*

The goal of this lesson is to develop a better understanding of what it means to listen actively but in a detached, non-reactive manner. It is so important to your husband's life, but this is also a skill that can greatly impact all of your relationships, especially your teenagers. You'll be given some practical ways to apply what you learned and will spend some time practicing. The work you put into this skill will pay dividends in your marriage and life.

5. **What to expect this week in the homework.**
We will learn the biblical understanding of listening and why we need to become a skilled listener. There are risks involved in marriage if we don't learn to listen to our husbands well. The main thing is what active-detached listening is and how to do it. There will be many practical exercises to practice this week, either with your husband or a friend. Next week we will do some practice exercises in class with partners, so be ready!

6. **Mini-assignment**
Find time to practice some of the listening skills you learned this week with either your husband, one of your children, or a friend. Be prepared to share.

7. **Prayer time.**

8. **Follow-up and communication.**

Session 9

1. **Open in prayer.**

2. **Greeting, Review Mini-Assignment** (10 minutes)
   Did you practice your listening skills you learned this week with someone this week?

3. **Review of Lesson 8 Homework—Chapter 9, Listening** (1 hour, 15 minutes)

Lesson 8 Discussion Questions

Day 1
1. (Q. 2-3) In the book, what was the problem with Susan? How do you relate to her? Is listening to your husband easy or difficult? Why?
2. (Q. 4) Why is one with a "quiet spirit" able to listen better?
3. (Q. 5, 6) Review Proverbs 18:13 and James 1:19-20. What does the Bible say about listening before answering?
4. (Q. 7, 8) What did we learn about the words "active" and "detached" as it pertains to listening? Describe active-detached listening.
5. F, F, T, T, T, F, T

Day 2
1. (Q. 2-4) What is the key idea in good listening? What is the goal? Why is it challenging?
2. (Q. 5) What are the risks of not listening well?
3. (Q. 6) What are five characteristics of good listening?
4. F, T, T, T, F, T
5. (Q. 7-13) Review 1 Timothy 3:11 and Proverbs 11:13. Discuss the questions.
6. (Q. 14-15) Was listening easier before marriage? Why or why not?
7. Review Marriage Exercise #1 on active, non-reactive techniques

Day 3 – See Listening Skills 101
1. (Q. 2) What do good listening techniques communicate?
2. (Q. 4-5) Eye contact questions. Practice time (3 minutes)
3. (Q. 6-8) Body language questions. Practice time (3 minutes)
4. (Q. 9-11) Minimal encouragers. Practice time (3 minutes)
5. (Q. 12-13) Verbal following. Practice time (3 minutes)

> **Day 4 - See Listening Skills 101**
> 1. (Q. 2-4) Ask follow-up questions. Practice time (3 minutes)
> 2. (Q. 5-7) Paraphrasing/reflecting back questions. Practice time (3 minutes)
> 3. (Q. 8-9) Summarizing. Practice time (5 minutes)
> 4. Marriage Exercise #2: Review scenarios.
>
> **Day 5**
> 1. (Q. 2) Describe what it means to maintain emotional distance when listening.
> 2. (Q. 3) How can we demonstrate that whoever we are listening to has our full attention?
> 3. (Q. 4-5) How should strong emotions be handled?
> 4. (Q. 6, 7) What do you and your husband do (or could do) to have undistracted listening times? Minimize distractions? See Marriage Exercise #3.
> 5. (Q. 8-10) What does it mean to have a sober mind when listening to your husband? How are men and women different in terms of talking?
>
> **Overall**
> Can anyone share their #1 take-a-way from this week's lesson?

4. **What to expect this week in the homework—Lesson 10, Conclusion**
   Lesson 9 is the conclusion and wrap-up to the study. It consists of only three days of homework but more time could be taken for reflection on Day 3. We will look at two stories, Beth and Regina, and reflect on what we can learn from them. Also, we will examine the opposite of a "Godly Wife" who we call the "Awful Wife." You'll be asked to use the skills you've learned each week to walk through some scenarios on what you could do to change this awful wife to a godly wife. Lastly, we are asking you to do a summarizing exercise on Day 3, which pulls each of the "#1 take-a-ways" from each week and puts them all on one page. You'll then prioritize the topics that are the most important for you to address and come up with some action items for the top three to get you started on the right track. Take this time to really think about all you've learned and what changes you've witnessed in your marriage since you've started putting some of the things from this study into practice.

5. **Mini-assignment**
   Reflection: Students should come prepared to share their #1 take away from each week's lesson next week (Day 3 homework).

6. **Prayer time.**

7. **Follow-up and communication.**

Listening Skills 101 – Practice Time

The following techniques are useful to communicate to others that you are interested in listening to them. They are simple but do require practice. (**Have students select a partner to practice with.**)

a. **Eye contact** —Active listening requires that you look at the speaker. It tells them that they are valuable and that you are listening. People can tell if you care or not by whether you look at them or look away. These are very powerful nonverbal clues.
   - Practice looking at your partner when she is talking.

b. **Body language**—When you are interested in what someone is saying, it is good to lean toward the person. The way your body leans is a huge signal about how much you want to listen.
   - Practice sitting across from your partner and lean toward her while she is talking at various times in the conversation. Give other positive body signals we learned in the lesson.

c. **Minimal encouragers**—These are the various grunts and groans, phrases, and expressions that tell another person you want them to keep talking. If none of these signals are given, it is extremely difficult to keep talking let alone go deeper. Examples to practice with your partner:
   - I hear you.
   - No!
   - Well!
   - Fascinating!
   - Really?
   - I don't believe it!
   - You don't say!
   - Oh!
   - Uh-huh.

d. **Verbal following**—This requires following the person's subject while she is talking and not switching topics to what her words remind you of or what you want to talk about. It takes a lot of self-discipline but think about how you feel when you are talking and the person jumps to a different, and maybe even unrelated topic! It can make you feel like you weren't heard.
   - Practice this with your partner now.

e. **Asking questions**—The skilled listener doesn't insert statements but asks a lot of questions. Asking questions says to the person, "You are important to me and I'm interested in what you want to talk about." Examples to practice:
   - What are you thinking about?
   - What are you feeling?
   - What do you think about _____?

- How is _____ going?
- Remember the last time we talked about _____? What happened with that?
- Have you had a chance to _____ lately?
- When someone is talking to you, instead of thinking about what you want to say next start formulating questions you can ask that will encourage the person to tell you more.
- When the subject is depleted, a new topic can be brought up.

f. **Paraphrase/reflecting back**—A helpful technique that means repeating the same words, or similar words, the person has just said. The key is to pick out emotional words and say them back to them. For example, if your husband says, "That guy really makes me angry!" you might say to him, "It sounds like you are really angry at this guy." Practice reflecting back and paraphrasing with your partner.

g. **Summarize**—Check to see if you heard correctly by saying, "Can I make sure I understood what you just said?" Give a quick, bulleted point recap – usually only about three thoughts at a time. This is an invitation to go deeper and give the person a chance to clarify and think through things he meant to say. Practice this with your partner.

Session 10

1. **Open in prayer.**

2. **Greeting, Review Mini-Assignment** (20 minutes)
   Share the #1 take away from each week's lesson next week. (Day 3 homework)

3. **Review of Lesson 9 Homework—Conclusion** (30 minutes)

Lesson 9 Discussion Questions

Day 1
1. (Q. 2) Discuss Beth's strategy about how she got her husband back. What would you do if you were in her situation?
2. (Q. 3) Discuss Regina and her marriage. What did you learn from her? Do you know a couple like this?
3. (Q. 4) What is your response to the quote given? How does this describe you? Has this changed any since you started this study?

Day 2
1. (Q. 2) Review the scenarios regarding the "Awful Wife." What would a godly wife do instead?

Day 3 – See Listening Skills 101
1. (Q. 2, 3) Share what order you put the categories in. What are some of the action items you plan to take for the top three priorities?

---

4. **Closing Remarks**
   - Remember, try not to get overwhelmed by all you've learned in this class. Focus on the top three areas you prioritized and work on them one at a time until it becomes more natural. Once you've mastered it, move on to the next area. Trust God and invite Him in. He will lead, guide, protect, and encourage you along the way.
   - Become a life-long student of your husband and what makes him happy. What can YOU do to help him be the godly man he is meant to be?
   - Make working on your marriage a lifetime priority. Honor God by honoring your husband. He is the man God gave you for life.

5. **Prayer time.**

Useful Resources for Marriage
By Gil Stieglitz

God's Radical Plan for Wives Companion Bible Study, by Jennifer Edwards. Nine lessons, perfect for individual or small group use.

God's Radical Plan for Husbands: Really Loving Your Wife

Marital Intelligence: A Foolproof Guide for Saving and Strengthening Marriage

Mission Possible: Winning the Battle Over Temptation

A complete list of resources is available at www.ptlb.com.

Other Resources
By Gil Stieglitz

Available in various formats from books to e-books, Kindle, audio, and podcasts. Check out www.ptlb.com for more information.

Becoming Courageous

Breaking Satanic Bondage

Deep Happiness: The 8 Secrets

Developing a Christian Worldview

Going Deep in Prayer: 40 Days of In-Depth Prayer

Leading a Thriving Ministry: 10 Indispensable Leadership Skills

Spiritual Disciplines of a C.H.R.I.S.T.I.A.N.

Intensive Training in Christian Spirituality

They Laughed When I Wrote Another Book About Prayer, Then They Read It: How to Make Prayer Work

Touching the Face of God: 40 Days of Adoring God

Why There Has to Be a Hell

Becoming a Godly Parent

Biblical Meditation: The Keys to Transformation

Everyday Spiritual Warfare

God's Guide to Handling Money

The 4 Keys to a Great Family

The Ten Commandments

If you would be interested in having Dr. Gil Stieglitz
come to speak to your group, you can contact him through the
Principles To Live By website:

www.ptlb.com

www.gilstieglitz.com

If you would like to have Jennifer Edwards
speak to your women's group, conduct a class or workshop,
or help with writing and editing needs,
you can contact her at her websites:

www.jenniferedwards.net

www.jedwardsediting.net

www.ingramcontent.com/pod-product-compliance
Lightning Source LLC
Chambersburg PA
CBHW080333170426
43194CB00014B/2552